Love in a Time of Caterpillars

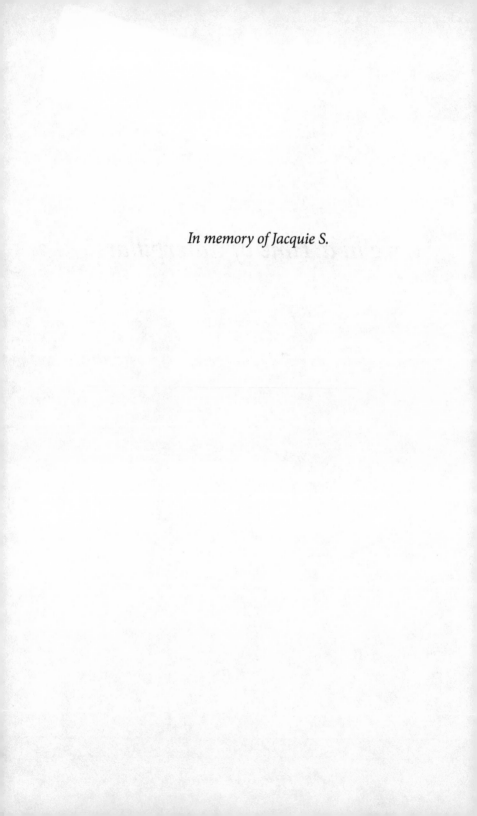

In memory of Jacquie S.

Love in a Time of Caterpillars

A Memoir of Monarchs and Caregiving

Allene Symons

Forked Road Press
Long Beach, California

Published 2024 by Forked Road Press

Cover design by Todd Crawshaw of Crawshaw Design
Photograph of the author by Kim Gottleib-Walker

Some names and identifying details have been changed. Where dialogue appears, the intention was to recreate the essence of conversations.

Trademarked names appear throughout this book. Forked Road Press recognizes all registered trademarks and service marks mentioned in this book.

"A Souvenir of Sunset Views" originally appeared in *Orange Coast* magazine.

Inquiries should be addressed to:
Forked Road Press
6285 E. Spring St. Box 414
Long Beach, CA 90808
714-745-2967
www.ForkedRoadPress.com

ISBN 978-0-9801165-7-1 (ebook)
ISBN 978-0-9801165-8-8 (paperback)

Printed in the United States of America

Table of Contents

Prologue

ONE DAY, IN EARLY 2021, I pulled off an intricate and tricky butterfly rescue. The small act of mercy reminded me of so many breath-catching moments when Alan and I had changed the fate of a single monarch.

During the past eight years of our quarter-century marriage, we'd welcomed hundreds and likely thousands of monarch visitors to our butterfly garden. They bestowed a gift of suspended time and a sorely needed distraction from the trials of Alan's unfolding dementia. Now, helping another butterfly in trouble was the least I could do. Pay it forward.

Monarchs gravitate to milkweed, their only host plant, where they lay their tiny eggs under or on top of a leaf, maybe in a cluster of buds. They first began arriving at our home in 2013 after we planted milkweed in a row along our driveway. Since then, butterflies have visited us from early spring through October. They were especially abundant during the ordeal of Alan's illness, which became apparent in 2017.

As his dementia progressed, the butterflies were unaware of how their presence—and especially the quirky antics of their caterpillars—turned moments of despair into distraction and delight. They gave us a sense of hope and purpose.

When it came to purpose, we knew we were helping the survival of a species under threat from human causes and climate change. We supplemented what nature provides yet commercial agriculture and development erase. By offering those visitors nectar plants for butterflies to sip and milkweed as food for their caterpillars, we increased the chance of one more creature fulfilling its life cycle, continuing the monarch's mission of migration and giving rise to the next generation.

But sometimes we went farther on the rare occasion when it became apparent that a monarch butterfly or caterpillar or chrysalis was in trouble. Sometimes it called for a small intervention.

Some say step aside and let nature take its course. This viewpoint became law in California in December of 2020, when the state Fish and Wildlife Service announced that it was listing the monarch as a protected species. Federal listing under the Endangered Species act is pending at the time I am writing this prologue in 2023. Who would not want them protected? Except this regulation included the provision that monarchs and their caterpillars could not be touched, could not be handled, except by accredited institutions. Technically, that ties the hands of thousands of us who provide home gardens for monarchs, as Alan and I did since 2013.

I hope the following account of one successful rescue, and the wider story of how monarchs helped us endure Alan's dementia, shows how sometimes a rule needs to be approached with nuance, danced around, sometimes given a gentle nudge.

The caterpillar I came upon this morning had chosen to form its chrysalis on a prime bit of pupa real estate—the red brick pillar on our front porch. So favored is this choice of the caterpillars that sometimes we've had a row of equally spaced chrysalises lined up like tiny dangling celadon green vases.

This one developing monarch was nearly ready to emerge (called eclose). I could see the orange and black wing pattern through the now-transparent skin of the chrysalis. The newbie was primed to meet the world … any minute, it seemed. I made it a point to delay my errands until a rise in morning temperature was likely to trigger this butterfly to make its debut. I waited a while to make sure it wasn't in trouble, and if so I would give it an assist.

Because it was a warm day, it appeared in the usual wing-crumpled way at about 9 a.m. Within a few minutes it had stretched open its wings, though they were not yet dried and set. It seemed perfectly formed, and I could identify its gender by the presence of two black spots in the lower area of each wing. Yes, it was a male.

Confident that in a couple of hours after drying and exercising his wings he would take off, I headed out for my errands and didn't return until midafternoon. I glanced to my left as I pulled into the driveway and neared the brick pillar on the porch, thinking he must be gone by now. But there he was.

How strange, I thought, because it wasn't a chilly day when a newly emerged butterfly might take longer to set its wings. Then I took a closer look … and saw that he was still attached, almost imperceptibly, to the chrysalis. One of his black antennae was stuck to the empty pupa case. For hours, it had tethered him there.

I'd never faced a problem like this in the nearly a decade since I'd been involved with monarchs, and now I wondered, what should I do? If he were here, what would my engineer husband have done in this situation? I tried to think, well, mechanically, I guess, about the problem, and it seemed that I should first establish a small space and a kind of tension between the butterfly and the chrysalis. I placed one finger near his legs and he climbed on, as they often seem willing to do, but he didn't move far because the tip of his antenna was still caught and holding him back.

With my other hand, I held onto the empty chrysalis and tried a gentle tug. But nothing happened. You're being too timid, I told myself, so I tried again. I attempted a more confident though riskier tug, and this time I pulled him free, antenna intact.

Next, I carried him to one of the wooden trellises where our newly emerged monarchs sometimes climb high to launch a maiden flight. I set him on a horizontal support about midway up, and right away, with his instinct to climb, he clambered to the top.

I went inside and watched through the kitchen window as he kept on working his wings. Resting, working, resting. This went on for quite a while, and becoming impatient, I left my window viewing spot and stepped outside. Perhaps it was the flurry of my arrival that spurred him to give a mighty thrust, and that's what he did, vaulting upward, catching a breeze, careening past the roofline and the orange tree, soaring away.

As the butterfly vanished into our neighborhood, my eyes followed him as far as I could see. I sent a grateful message into the universe ... as if Alan could hear:

We did it again, my dear. Another one saved.

Chapter 1
RULES FOR SURVIVAL

Welcome to Our Group

THE VISITING MONARCHS were our therapy partners, but another coalition was the monthly support group of my local branch of the Alzheimer's Association.

Family caregivers who join such support groups soon discover that there are prescribed rules for caring for a loved one with dementia: Don't remind them they forgot. Do repeat instructions or sentences in exactly the same way. Don't reason. Don't argue. And the one that perhaps hits me hardest now, for the many reasons it applies: Do use the power of touch.

Our monthly sharing and discussion sessions were moderated by a certified leader from the Alzheimer's Association. One piece of her advice looms large: We cannot take care of our loved ones unless we take care of ourselves. In my group, many of us are taking care of spouses, and given our age, that advice comes with a flagged warning. Statistics vary in different studies, but a significant percentage of those caring for a spouse with dementia will die before their afflicted mate.

I'd like to take you back to the summer of 2019. When I reach the telling incident, you might wonder if I broke one of those rules. I would rather call it a workaround.

Tuesday, July 9, 2019. My Alzheimer's support group beckons like a two-hour vacation, a respite from the strain of my role as a caregiver-wife. I sink into a padded folding chair in this familiar room in the community center and my shoulders begin to relax. I am with kindred spirits. Today there are twenty-four of us, almost all female and mostly spouses. We are seated on both sides of a U-shaped, pushed-together island of tables. My island getaway.

Our facilitator, whom I'll call Audrey—I think of her as our coach—moderates these sessions. Because she has decades of experience in dementia care, her advice is delivered with empathy, humor, and tough love. She sits at the head of the longest of the three tables. Light from a window glints on her short silver hair.

The support group combines education with therapy and provides a kind of catharsis, but the heart of the meetings is about sharing our latest experiences. This leads to discussions of the problems we raise. They vary from how to stop an afflicted loved one from driving, to what if they begin to wander and risk getting get lost. We talk about the powerful tools of distraction and redirection to steer them away from repetition or obsession. Or worse. And, of course, about how we feel when we fail at the toughest tool of all, summoning our own increasingly scarce supply of patience.

Now that we've all signed the attendance sheet the meeting begins, and in terms of sequence, you never know which of us Audrey will call on next. It's much like the unpredictability of the disease itself. Because I am sitting near the head of the table, Audrey turns her head my way and asks, "So, Allene, what's going on in your life?"

I describe what happened when we were eating our Sunday at-home brunch alongside an array of newspapers, which these days my mate likes to glance through but no longer reads.

"My husband," I say, "couldn't remember my name." I tell

them about his agitated struggle to find the missing word, how he'd said, "I know you're my wife. But don't tell me your name—let me work it through."

I'd watched him flounder, with both of us helpless, until suddenly an image came to mind. "I saw it like a little scene," I tell the group, "so this is what I said to him. 'When we first met, we exchanged business cards, and both of us noticed how unusual it was that our names are so similar.' He brightened with 'I remember now—your name is Allene!'"

I end this installment of what's-going-on-in-my-life by saying we'd broken the tension by taking a short stroll along our monarch garden. "Afterward, he seemed calm, and so we went on with our Sunday breakfast." This is how another marker of dementia, forgetting my name, had surfaced while I was simply spreading my toast with peach jam.

As I write this, it has been almost four years since I first suspected that my husband had dementia. After fretting about what to do, I had convinced him to take a preliminary test by making a proposition: "I want to take this screening test for myself, so let's both take it as a benchmark. Then we'll go out for lunch."

That turned out to be one of my most dependable ploys: try to include a treat. What comes before the treat might need to be sugarcoated, too, with the phrasing the Alzheimer's Association calls a "loving lie." New people who join our support group balk at the idea at first, but eventually they accept the necessity of fibbing to a loved one for everyone's sake. Learn the art of doing it well.

I am fairly new here, compared to veteran members of the

support group, some of whom have endured their continuing caregiver role for a decade or more. By July of 2019, it has been a year since I joined this group.

Along with the experienced or veteran members are those Audrey calls "the alumni," the people who have already lost their loved one. The ordeal, if not their grief, is now in the past, but they continue to attend the support group to help others.

For her part, our Alzheimer's Association leader has heard of just about every imaginable situation during her decades as a dementia-care professional. Wary of pat answers, she fields discussion of possible solutions and lays out multiple choices to questions such as How do you know, or when do you know, or can you ever know with certainty that it is time to place your loved one in a memory care facility?

Among those attending today's support group are two first-timers who listen as we take turns around the table. Toward the end of the session Audrey asks one, "Do you feel like speaking, or would you rather not?" and the 50-something woman takes a deep breath, and says, "Yes, I would."

"I saw a chart of Alzheimer's stages on the Internet," she continues, "and I'm here because I want to pin down my mother's degree of progression. I want to know what comes next." And she adds, "What to expect."

A chart may simplify this complex disease into phases, but the actuality is far from straightforward. This is why, as stated in literature from the Mayo Clinic: Depending on the area of the brain that's affected, dementia can affect people differently and cause different symptoms.

Dementia often begins with difficulty finding words, yet such forgetfulness can also result from depression or a response to medication or simply be a function of aging. If symptoms persist and increase, however, then it is likely attributable to Alzheimer's, which accounts for around eighty percent of dementia cases. There are other forms of dementia, too, as I would later learn as my husband's illness progressed.

Some patients retain high functioning, maybe even a narrow reserve, a niche, of strength. At this time in mid-2019, my husband is still considered highly cognitive. This former engineer and math professor has many outward symptoms of dementia, among them difficulty getting dressed and even writing his name, yet he is articulate and retains an impressive recall of scientific facts. During one of my support group meetings, I heard about a woman with advanced dementia who could still vanquish anyone at Scrabble. This is why the what-to-expect question is so slippery.

After several years of living with this process, I can attest to why it is hard for family members to get a handle on dementia. It can be months or years before you receive a diagnosis beyond the early stage of mild cognitive impairment (MCI). At this time, no magic diagnostic bullet yet exists for pinning down Alzheimer's. Also hard to pin down are the two major variants, frontotemporal dementia (ten to fifteen percent of cases) and Lewy body dementia (about twenty percent). Those don't add up to one hundred, like a pie chart spilling over with possibilities.

So here you are, perhaps a wife like me with a husband in what might be in the early stage of dementia, and you know—yet do not know—what is happening to him. For now, what do we call it? What can we expect?

The easy answer is to call it Alzheimer's, the most common form of dementia, and this term serves as a sad but handy label. Even before receiving a diagnosis, it communicates that this is not a temporary condition, not an occasion for a get-well card.

But there is another kind of card, resembling a business card, provided by the Alzheimer's Association and intended for us to carry along to stores, restaurants, and social settings. The card reads: "Please be patient. The person I am with has Alzheimer's."

Meanwhile, back to the same Tuesday at the community center. It is now five p.m., when after discussion of how the chart of stages only serves as a rough guide, Audrey closes with a question: "How could anyone write a book about Alzheimer's?" She means there is no one way, not one definitive perspective.

Many books have been written on this subject and others will follow. As a writer who is also a spousal caregiver, this is my take on the experience. I have kept a journal, and from its pages I hope to contribute to a mosaic of understanding. Every caregiver's experience is unique, but I believe that some universal insights can be gleaned from one family's particular story.

And that is my goal in writing this narrative account, not only about the dark times occasioned by this disease, and how I handled those as best I could, but also how a closing curtain sometimes opens to reveal bright moments.

For us, these times most often take place when we are tending to our monarch butterfly garden.

At the time I am writing this chapter, he seems to be in a mid-stage of as-yet-unspecified dementia. We are still in a manageable stage, but I know this phase will pass. He has a terminal disease. At some point, like others in my support group, I will begin to experience what is known as anticipatory grief. For now, I cling to the present and I treasure our past.

The Way We Were

LATELY, WHEREVER WE GO, I discretely take several Alzheimer's clue-people-in cards. On the day Alan and I met almost three decades ago, there were business cards involved, too. We later disagreed about the circumstances, not the time or place, but what to call it. Over the years, if people asked, he would say, "We met in a bar. I was drinking a glass of pinot," and I would counter with, "No, it was a café, and I was drinking iced tea." As supporting evidence, I'd offer, to anyone interested in knowing the backstory, that I was a bookstore manager on my *dinner break*.

That day we met came three years after I'd moved back to Southern California following a decade of working in the publishing industry in New York. The concern that brought me home was to be close at hand for my elderly mother; the job that brought me home was a position as general manager of a bookstore in South Coast Plaza, an upscale Southern California shopping complex.

Rizzoli International Bookstore is the retail branch of the Italian art and architecture book publisher. It's one of those stores with rich wooden shelves where you browse while trendy European hits ("What is that? I must buy it!") and classical music or operatic arias play in the background.

I was on an early dinner break one afternoon in 1991 when I first noticed Alan. We couldn't miss each other, the only two customers in the café. It was off-hours, too late for lunch but too early for the dinner crowd, and the tables sat empty. A single server tended to customers at the marble counter. We were sitting a few feet apart on our long-legged stools. First of all, I liked his professorial look, this tall, slim man who wore glasses and had a trim beard. Second, I decided he must like books because a bag from my store sat on his lap.

Curious about what he'd bought, I was not yet curious enough to ask. I also had a shopping bag because I'd hastily made a purchase at the beginning of my dinner break. The server, who knew me as a regular, gave us an opening.

"What did you buy at Macy's?" she asked.

"A coffee maker," I said. "Mine died this morning."

From my left, down the counter, the stranger spoke: "Is it digital or analog?"

"Digital or analog?"—a reminder that for consumers, 1991 was still early in the era of digital devices. "I'm not sure," I replied. "I was in a hurry when I bought it." I dug into my bag, pulled out the box, and held it up. It had a clock face, two hands.

"Analog," he said. "Good choice. Likely to be fewer complications."

I liked his offered tidbit of fact, and our exchange progressed from there. Soon I asked him what he'd purchased and he said a psychology book. "I took too many psych classes in college, I suppose, though I ended up as a civil engineer with a specialty in rivers. Hydrology."

He handed me a business card and I handed one back.

"Store manager?" he said. "I didn't see you there."

"I spend a lot of time in the back office," I replied. I looked at his card, which had the Orange County seal and read Flood Control. "I suppose you don't have much to do these days, California being in a drought."

A sly smile. "You've heard of a hundred-year flood? I've seen footage of houses falling into a flooded creek not far from here. That was in the 1960s."

I felt embarrassed by my scientific stupidity so I switched topic. "Which book did you buy." He pulled one out of the Rizzoli bag, a book about working through relationships, and though I wasn't about to ask, he explained, "I recently went through a break-up with a girlfriend and I'm trying to get my head back together."

A few minutes of conversation followed, then a half hour later, I looked at my watch. "Well, I'm expected back at the store."

"Before you leave, may I ask … are you seeing someone?" My answer was to write my home phone number on my card.

When we'd met that day on my dinner break at Rizzoli, I was able to glean from our conversation that though he was a science guy, he wasn't only a geek like my engineer dad. Alan had an interest in the arts. Theater. Opera. *An engineer? Do not hit reject,* my inner gatekeeper said.

He called a day later and asked me to dinner the following week. "I'd love to," I said, "but I'll be in New York." I was scheduled to appear on NBC's *Today Show*, talking about my new travel book *Adventures Abroad*. It was based on interviews with fifty American expats who had retired in different countries. I was the co-author along with retirement-abroad expert Jane Parker. She and I had practiced succinct replies to the possible questions that might be thrown at us by the *Today Show* hosts, as if we were preparing to defend ourselves in court. Our preparation helped us walk confidently out of the Green Room and onto the set for our interview, a nerve-wracking but exhilarating experience. Turned out, Alan had taped the show.

After I returned home, he and I had our first date at an Indian restaurant named Gandhi. We talked about the past and the present, our mutual interest in photography and Scuba diving, and our hopes for the future. This all transpired in an invisible cloud of spices, of cumin and turmeric, coriander and cardamom, as if it were a predictor of years of world travel and exploration ahead. And though Gandhi eventually changed ownership, we would celebrate our anniversary there every year for the next quarter century of our shared life.

After a weekday dinner on our second date, he invited me to see his home. Still in the early dating mode of driving my own car, I pulled to the curb out front and couldn't miss the huge ash tree, looming like a landmark in the deep setback of his front yard. I had no idea how much this tree would play a joyful, yet threatening, role in our future life together.

Sheltered From Harm

IT SO HAPPENS THAT in nature a tiny percentage of monarchs survive the five stages from egg to butterfly. For the past several years, though, the offspring that have landed in our garden have enjoyed much better odds. This is because our occasional caterpillar interventions improve the chances of survival for those in our care. Sometimes we move one from a stripped-bare milkweed to another plant lush with leaves. At times we flick off an advancing wolf spider or swat way a wasp. We cannot eradicate all the predators, but we can redirect a caterpillar, rippling along on its little legs, away from trouble and out of harm's way.

Harm's way. It sneaks up on you.

The signs of dementia can appear and disappear like vapor and arise in unlikely situations. In the summer of 2016, Alan's daughter, Cathy, along with her husband and our two grandkids (my step-grandkids), visited us in Southern California. For our annual vacations, we make it a resort week rather than hanging around at the grandparents' house lacking in amenities. Instead, we go to a kid-friendly hotel, and that summer it was a week at the Hilton resort in San Diego.

The plan for one day was for him to go Scuba diving with his daughter. I stayed behind and read a book by the pool so they could have their father-daughter time together, but when they returned that afternoon Cathy took me aside.

"Maybe my dad is getting forgetful," she said. She'd been surprised to see him having trouble using the gauges and indicators and the controls for buoyancy. He'd also made an ascent to the surface too fast for safety. It concerned her because he was such an experienced diver, as was she.

I said I had noticed a few instances of short-term forgetfulness, and we talked about possibilities. One might be a return of depression because he had undergone periods of this in the past, so with the two of us urging him, Alan reluctantly agreed to see a recommended psychiatrist.

For several months he saw this specialist, who placed him on an anti-depressant. The memory issues continued, though, and he became increasingly repetitive and evasive in sessions. I know this because occasionally the doctor would plan a joint session with both of us. In time, the shape of Alan's illness began to emerge.

A further insight occurred the next time we saw our primary care physician for a wellness visit. As a senior couple, for the past couple of years we had opted for joint rather than separate appointments. We felt that we were there to cover each other's back, to make sure we followed up on the doctor's instructions.

At the next appointment with our primary care physician, when I mentioned Alan's tendency to be forgetful, he gave my husband a routine cognitive "wellness" test. It involved several questions, such as the date, the city where he lives, the season of the year, and who is the current president. Alan missed the mark on one or two answers but made excuses. The doctor said, in an aside to me, that we would take a wait-and-see approach. Meanwhile, the psychiatrist, who saw him more frequently than the internist, was becoming concerned about his repetitive, looping stories.

Then came a new year, and in February of 2017 I attended a conference in San Francisco. I had a new book out, *Aldous Huxley's Hands*, and was a speaker on two panels. But I worried about Alan, whom I'd left at home alone that entire weekend, even though I had no specific reason for concern, not even about his driving. Not yet.

Around this same time an item appeared in a column by Steve Lopez in the *Los Angeles Times*, about a missing woman who suffered from dementia. The husband had lost his wife during an outing to the Los Angeles County Museum of Art. He went into a restroom, and when he came out she was gone. Vanished. She had disappeared without her purse, meaning no ID.

This was a chilling scenario, and even if it did not yet apply to my husband, my thoughts raced ahead to future sojourns: What if someday Alan and I were separated in another city, or even in Los Angeles, and he wandered off? He was already starting to have trouble with his iPhone. I might not be able to reach him. He might lose his iPhone. I might lose him.

And how much riskier it would be if he and I were separated in a foreign city far from home. In recent years, I'd written travel articles that were published with his photographs, about cruising the Danube, exploring Paris, island hopping from a liveaboard boat in the Galapagos. Now I was scheduled for another out-of-town conference, this one in relation to my new book at the bienni al Aldous Huxley conference in Spain. Alan was planning to come with me but on the psychiatrist's advice, I cancelled. Travel had been a central theme in our marriage, now, it appeared, travel was a thing of the past.

Although our family doctor was taking a wait-and-see approach to Alan's memory issue, I was becoming impatient for a diagnosis. This is a frequent complaint by new members of my support group. Is what they are observing in their spouse or parent a normal sign of aging, a side effect of meds or depression, or are we talking about Alzheimer's, a terminal disease?

I lit up when I saw a newspaper announcement for an affordable dementia assessment test. To enlist Alan's cooperation, I suggested that we both take the Memory Assessment available at the Hoag Neuroscience Institute in Newport Beach, not far from where we live. On appointment day, we took a scenic route with a view of the Pacific, as I was already angling to make any outing related to his health as pleasurable as possible. Alan drove, enjoying the new 2017 Toyota RAV 4 he'd purchased that March. When we arrived at Hoag, I was pleased to see that, unlike a stark clinic, the facility gave the impression of a tastefully appointed hotel.

When our names were called, we each took a turn, and I went first. The assessment, which took place inside a small room, was a process that involved recalling the names of objects along with some descriptive words. A 50 percent score is the dividing line for normal. When Alan emerged from the room and showed me the printed results, I saw that his score came out at 30 percent. I didn't mention that mine was 80. He seemed unconcerned, but to me his score seemed shockingly low. It occurred to me that maybe he had been mustering his high IQ to hide his condition for far longer than I'd imagined.

Memory lapses and losing things continued, but so did our everyday life.

Come July, it was time for my every-five-year colonoscopy, with its unpleasant examination prep. Throughout our marriage, we had accompanied each other to this important recurring exam, one of us driving the twilight-anesthesia-incapacitated partner home. Driving there was no problem on that Friday, and Alan read a book for the duration in the waiting room. Afterward, as is typical, I was so groggy that instructions and a scheduled time for a follow-up could not possibly register with me, so as usual, this information and a printed sheet were conveyed to my spouse.

But come Monday, I received a phone call from the physician's office. I had an appointment. Had I forgotten? "I can be there in ten minutes," I said, then turned to my husband. "The doctor's office said I had a follow-up appointment today and I didn't know. Where is the follow up sheet that they gave you?"

"I don't remember and I have no idea where it is," he said, as I headed for the door. Driving myself back to the medical office in my little red car, at first I thought, *Okay, I should have asked my husband about the follow-up*, but this had always been a team effort, one of us attaching the after-care sheet on the refrigerator with a magnet, or maybe setting it in clear sight on the kitchen counter. My second thought was that maybe I could no longer rely on him. He had always been there for me, my rock, but it struck me that I was now standing exposed and on my own. Three days later, I began keeping a detailed journal.

His forgetting to mention my follow-up instructions, combined with his Hoag assessment results of three months ago, gave his daughter Cathy cause to be concerned for my welfare. She needed me to remain healthy to care for him. So did I, because she lived two thousand miles away.

As months passed, she began to advance the idea of hiring support to ensure that I was taking adequate care of myself. This idea had two aspects. One was home care assistance, perhaps starting with a few hours per week. But I said it was way too early, that I didn't need assistance and, moreover, her dad would flat out reject any outsider.

The other aspect was the possibility that, at some vague future time, he might require placement in a memory care facility. I was learning more about this approach to treatment in my Alzheimer's support group, where some members had home care help and others had spouses or parents living in facilities. Yet the very word *placement* struck me as ominously final. My Plan A was to keep my husband at home.

After all, I was managing and took pride in that fact. I was barely in my seventies, and Alan was a couple of years older. With continued vigilance, I expected it would continue working out for both of us because he and I still had our cozy if increasingly modified routine. Sharing meals was one of the everyday anchors in our life, and we watched nightly news during dinner. We enjoyed lunch on the patio when the weather allowed and looked forward to our at-home Sunday brunches accompanied by an array of newspapers.

We also attended off-hour movies when the crowds were sparse and went to a favorite restaurant, where the manager and our regular server knew about Alan's condition. We had our health club, where he swam downstairs while I practiced Pilates for the same hour upstairs. By now I had cancelled our regional theater subscription, because he could no longer follow a narrative; I had likewise cancelled our membership in the L.A. County Museum of Art, because it would be too easy for him to wander away in the large multi-building complex. But there were substitutes, like the small and jewel-like Bowers Museum, just a few blocks from our home and a place where Alan couldn't possibly get lost.

This period of our life was still in some ways, I kept convincing myself, the best of times.

Thanks to my support group and from reading what I call the Alzheimer's Association "rules," I was learning countless ways to ensure his safety. But even if I followed them to the letter, which is impossible, I did not want to become a statistic: an exhausted, health impacted spousal caregiver who pre-deceases their mate. If something happened to me, or if adding home care eventually proved insufficient, then he might need to be *placed*—I shuddered to call it committed—in a memory care facility.

I'd begun to notice more ads for senior living on the TV, on the internet, and in print publications, so I began to stretch past my Plan A as I thought: *Well, maybe for his sake we might move into a senior complex*—the kind that included memory care. The memory care section (I naively thought) would be just a stroll down the hall from my independent-living apartment. We would have dinners together, right? Wrong. But I didn't know it then.

Around this same time, in the fall of 2017, construction began on a large development a couple of miles from our home. A *Coming Soon* sign appeared announcing Oakmont Senior Living. Independent, Assisted Living, Memory Care. It seemed like an omen pointing toward Plan B. At a minimum, this was an excuse to bring Al with me in the guise of curious neighbors, so I signed up for the email list.

In January of 2018 I received an invitation to the pre-opening and RSVP'd for two. This was Al's first taste, and quite literally a taste, because at the opening they served delicious and sophisticated small plates and beverages in the sparkling new dining room. Oakmont had a small garden, a gym, a game room, and a theater for showing recent films.

"It's kind of like a cruise ship," he said, having at that time no idea that this might be a possibility for us. Then I saw a way to run with his favorable impression to enable me to look at other facilities. "I might pitch a magazine article about places like this," I said. "It's a coming trend, with a wave of elderly Baby Boomers." My byline had appeared on many magazine articles over the years, including trend pieces, so he didn't question my plan. Plus, he'd always enjoyed tagging along on my staff-writer and freelance research trips.

Soon we had visited a few of these three-tier facilities masquerading as cruise ships perpetually in port. If I heard about another one with good ratings that we hadn't seen, he was glad to check it out. He even began critiquing features, especially if it had a pool—length, sun exposure—and I could see he was beginning to imagine us living in such a setting. Sampling senior facilities was turning into a travel adventure. Now that we could no longer explore the world, we had embarked on a Land Cruise.

When it came to visiting a memory care section, always secured from the rest of these facilities to prevent wandering, I made sure this was the briefest stop on the itinerary. Not wanting to alarm Alan by his catching sight of residents in advanced stages of dementia, I'd tell the marketing person who showed us around, "I'll just poke my head in for a minute."

At one facility, which featured spacious balconies on some of the independent units, he asked the person who had us in tow, "We have a sanctuary garden for monarch butterflies. Would we be able to keep planter boxes out here?"

"Plants on the balcony in pots?" said our marketing escort. "No problem."

Three years before this, however, our Monarch Project had begun with a problem.

We'd established the garden in 2013 by purchasing a few gallon containers of milkweed plants at our local nursery. But within a few hours a startling number of caterpillars began to emerge from their tiny egg cases. Within two days we had twenty-eight yellow-and-black striped caterpillars, all chomping away on the milkweed.

"I am amazed at how much joy this brings," my husband said as we surveyed our substantial herd. But then came alarm because soon they had consumed away nearly all the leaves, and milkweed is their only acceptable food. This was the season when monarch enthusiasts refresh their gardens, and our nursery had no milkweed left. Calls determined that other sources were also out of stock.

That was a hard lesson about managing a shelter garden, trying to improve on nature's odds but finding it would be more challenging than we'd anticipated. We counted on maybe fending off predators like spiders, not that the food we provided would become scarce. Guilt set in. What if our caterpillars starved because of our poor planning?

But as with any kind of caregiving, once you're committed you try to do your best.

Luckily, the leaf-shortage crisis during our first monarch springtime had a happy ending. Even as more eggs hatched, ratcheting up our anxiety, we stumbled on our first successful attempt at intervention: We relocated caterpillars, gently plucking them from one leaf and setting them down on another so the consumption rate between plants balanced out, an approach that bought us time until a new shipment arrived at the nursery.

For me, it was an epiphany about the life-saving potential of the *workaround*. It was one of my first monarch-inspired insights, and one I would apply when my husband's dementia began to emerge three years later.

In the larger scheme of things, dementia and butterfly statistics veer in opposite directions: Monarchs are in decline, dementia cases are on the rise. By the middle of the twenty-first century, the current estimate of five million dementia patients is projected to swell to fourteen million, expanded by the aging Baby Boom demographic.

By 2018, I would realize that I had not one but two missions. By then, Alan and I would be deeply committed to doing our part for the monarch preservation movement, even if our garden was just a tiny dot on the globe. The other mission, or call it another purpose in life, would be my advocacy for dementia outreach.

For my husband, even as his ability declined, some reservoirs of strength showed no sign of decreasing. As a former lifeguard and former Army medic, his affinity for helping others, whether human or butterfly, so far remained intact.

No matter how uncertain life seemed, when we walked in the garden and came upon one of our tiny striped caterpillars, the promise of their transformation brought us close in a circle of compassion for all living things.

Chapter 2
ROAD TRIP

I'll Drive, She Said

In January of 2018, the same month Alan and I toured the new senior complex called Oakmont, I hatched another plan. It had been several months since the Hoag memory assessment, and by now I had begun to see cracks in Alan's driving technique.

"Honey," I told him one day, "with the Hoag memory assessment results rather low, I think you should limit your driving to local places."

"My driving skills are excellent!"

I didn't want to push the point that he'd been involved in an accident the previous year because it had been deemed not his fault. "But the Hoag test showed that you have a short-term memory issue," I said. "You might experience a lapse of judgment."

We haggled back and forth for a while until I added, "Someone could get hurt."

That phrase caught his attention, my husband the former lifeguard. "Okay, okay. I'll try it. Local only," he said with a sulk.

The next day, as if to exercise this range of motion to the max, he drove by himself to four different stores. Afterward, he listed them aloud: Trader Joe's, Ace Hardware, Armstrong Nursery, and the World Market, a sprawling place crammed with imported goods. All told, he was gone for three hours, and by the time he got home, clutching several bags, he was so worn out from the excursion that he crawled under a quilt and took a nap.

"Being exhausted isn't safe, either," I told him after his siesta. I was frustrated. How could I limit his driving before something happened, like maybe him dozing off behind the wheel? But I didn't want to take away his privileges, either. Not entirely. They meant so much to him. How could I preserve some of his love of mechanical momentum?

I'd say that driving—the danger of a dementia patient roaming free-range behind the wheel of a large vehicle—is the top worry when a new member joins our support group. The prospect of giving up a driver's license after many decades of independence, especially for a man, is painful not only for the driver himself but for any family member involved in the process. But it has to be dealt with. Danger trumps a mate's outrage at getting his wings clipped. Bluntly stated, a dementia patient is likely to crash into another car or a pole or hit a pedestrian. It's a matter of life and death. And liability.

Each experienced member of the support group had a different twist on how they handled this problem. We shared our stories with the newbies, detailing how we gradually finagled away a

driver's license despite facing, in the loved one's view, the accusa-
tion of You stole it from me! Typically, this process of making the
call happens in phases and is not an effort made by the mate alone,
but a combination of spouse and doctor and, finally, the Department of Motor Vehicles.

The story I share with new members similarly involves several steps. The first one, his reluctant agreement to limit himself to
local-only driving, did not ensure safety. That step would require
the word of someone with authority, like our family doctor, and
though that may sound definitive, it took months of back and forth
at medical appointments.

This is because the stop-driving challenge reflects a core
problem—a diagnosis of dementia is not easy to pin down. Never-
theless, I had to act. I informed our primary care physician about
the initial memory-assessment results at the Hoag clinic (our doctor is affiliated with a different medical group), and booked an office visit. Once we were there, the doctor again asked Alan a few
simple questions of the "What is the date" and "Remember this
word" variety. Alan faltered on about half the answers.

At one point in the visit, the doctor asked me to step outside
the room. Standing in the hallway, he asked me, "Isn't it time for
your husband to give up driving?" But he was not insistent, and I
had not yet seen Alan manifest any scary driving habits, so I replied, "I don't think so. It's still too soon." I was reluctant to take
away his freedom.

A few months later, though, two worrisome signs began to
appear. One was a twitchy reaction to cars in Alan's peripheral vision, such as when another car made a legal turn nearby. Then he

twice missed one of our usual freeway off-ramps, though I had alerted him about the upcoming exit. He dismissed his error with "Guess I wasn't paying attention."

Oh, well, I thought, I've done that myself.

Then a month or so later, his jerky reaction on surface streets increased. I watched him flinch when he saw pedestrians walking parallel to us on the sidewalk, as if they posed a driving hazard to *him*. It was the beginning of a perceptual problem that would have more serious manifestations later on.

Around the same time, he also took a few wrong turns on familiar surface streets, such as while driving to our dentist. The first time I pointed this out he said he'd just been distracted. The next time he flared at me. "I made that turn because I wanted to make that turn!"

He had morphed into a rebel. His wrongs became rights.

Now I faced a greater problem, and I needed to enlist back-up. His daughter Cathy arranged for a week's visit during her spring break from teaching, a trip mainly to see her dad. It was also a chance for the two of us to talk about future plans and … gently gang up on Alan about his driving.

During her stay, he was behind the wheel as the three of us ran around town to dine out or pick up groceries or catch a film. Sitting in the back seat, she pointed out driving errors, and though he became irritated, I gained leverage from her comments. Eventually on one outing, I turned to her and, summing up my major concern, said, "I think your dad is being physically reactive to what's going on around him." I saw his hand tightly grip the steering wheel, but I continued with my riff. "I don't want him driving alone on the freeway because I've seen him miss exits, and I'm afraid he might overcompensate and cause a crash."

From the back seat came "I agree."

We expected him to be mad at us, but at least she and I had shared the brunt of his outrage. And, yes, he felt ganged-up on, but he knew that in all the world we were the two people whose love could be counted on. Always. Which we pointed out to him, repeatedly. Faced with this force of affection and insistence and worn down by our pleas, he reluctantly agreed not to take the freeway unless I was in the car with him.

Avoiding the freeway was a good second step, I thought. Except it turned out to be unenforceable.

After Cathy returned to her husband and kids in suburban Chicago, and not long after our family decision about her dad's driving, aka Phase Two, I became suspicious about his observance of the no-freeway rule. One day he told me he planned to run an errand later that afternoon, so out of curiosity I noted the odometer mileage. He took off and after quite a long time, over an hour, he returned home.

"How'd it go?" I asked.

"I took my time, looking at sale items at Harbor Freight," he said, referring to a hardware discount store a couple of miles away, one easily reached via surface streets. The odometer, though, told a different story. He surely had taken the freeway much, much farther than Harbor Freight. *Busted.*

I challenged him. And he denied it. I mentioned the odometer. I proposed that he drive only with me in the car. I reminded him that our doctor had already raised the prospect that he stop driving entirely. But, I added, I was his advocate. "I defended you to the doctor," I said. "I told him it was not yet time to give up driving."

That *not yet* loomed over us like a cloud.

Reluctantly, Alan agreed that he would only drive with me.

Those were often angry rides, full of recrimination and mur-murings of "I am being treated like a child." It next occurred to me that maybe he took the SUV out alone while I was running an er-rand in my little red car, so I wanted to find out if this was the case. A tool in the care-giving kit when your mate has dementia, and a powerful companion to the loving lie, is ... spying.

Soon I conjured an excuse and pulled my red Honda Fit out of the driveway and waited two blocks south, knowing that if he took the white SUV, he could only turn north on our divided street. While waiting, I thought back to something I'd done when I was a teenager. My parents would go out for an evening, taking one of the two family cars. No sooner than they were gone, I'd sneak out with the other car, using one of my surreptitiously cop-ied duplicate keys. I had a new license then, but not their permis-sion to drive at night. I just drove around the block a few times, but it felt like a thrill nonetheless. Remembering this, I realized that dealing with a dementia patient is like dealing with a troublesome teenager. Sure enough—within minutes he pulled the SUV down the driveway. I didn't try to stop him. He was still a legal driver.

Instead, I needed a workaround. It happened that I had use of an empty garage space at a family property a few miles away, so I fibbed and told him my car needed extensive repairs. "I am thinking about replacing it," I said, and I arranged for a friend to follow me so I could drop off my car then she brought me back "from the shop."

Meanwhile, I told Alan that, for a while at least, we would be a one-car family and share his car. He thought it was temporary when we began going out together in the SUV, still mainly with him driving, but soon he started crabbing that it seemed like he couldn't go anywhere by himself.

I continued to shrink his options.

My little red car never came home because I sold it. I was very fond of that car, which I'd so carefully chosen and conscientiously maintained in cherry condition. I was sad to see it go, but I had to say goodbye. Change was upon us, and it was on my shoulders to serve as the change agent. When I told him I'd sold my car ("Oh, it was old and needed too many repairs"), I offered a sweet trade-off. "The advantage now is that you can use my half of the garage for your workshop," I said. "It'll be like having your own Man Cave." This idea immediately appealed to him. He didn't understand or know we were one step closer to the end of his adult lifetime of driving.

Riding shotgun on surface streets, I soon noticed a further increase in his sudden lurching reactions. When I yelped, he claimed people were stepping off the curb and he was being cautious, but I was watching carefully and could see that this was a false perception. I had to take a more drastic step.

Alan was unaware when I called the doctor and told him about my husband's increasingly odd perception of people appearing in his peripheral vision. The doctor insisted on an appointment the following day. When we arrived, he went through a few of the short-term memory questions, most of which Alan failed. "Alan," the doctor said, "I'm afraid it's time for you to give up driving. As your doctor, it is my responsibility to notify the Department of Motor Vehicles." Thankfully, the bad news didn't come from me.

Within a week or two, a letter addressed to Alan arrived from the DMV. I sneakily opened it. Inside was a notice of cancellation of his license, but it included a form if he wanted to challenge the decision. Now, I knew he still had cognitive capacity and an amazing retention of facts, even if he didn't know what month it was. I pictured him rising to the occasion, passing a driving test, then letting down his guard, exhausted and barely able to drive safely home. Somehow that DMV form became … well, let's say it was waylaid in a pile of junk mail. Or let's say I kept the form but failed to mention it. (I figured, so sue me.) And have I mentioned omission as a subset of loving lies?

After the letter incident and my scant remorse about being a scofflaw, his ability further deteriorated. Now there was no doubt in my mind. Ending his driving life was clearly the right decision for everyone's sake. But when a dementia patient, and perhaps more so a man, is forced to give up driving, the resentment can linger and burrow underground. For Alan, giving up driving led to another kind of rebellion. Unknown to me, he had placed an online order for a heavy-duty electric tricycle.

Epiphany at the DMV

IT SEEMED that Alan had, at last, accepted the official decree that he was no longer capable of driving a car, and it hadn't required an accident. This epiphany surfaced at the Department of Motor Vehicles on the day of his appointment to obtain his Senior ID.

By then, his driver's license, which I had in my possession, had been invalid for months, but with no reason such as air travel we hadn't taken steps to obtain an alternate ID. Didn't see any rush. The problem is, when a license is invalid, if you keep the old one and casually try to use it for any kind of identification, you'll run into trouble.

We ran into this situation because of an old safe in the basement. He had owned this safe for years, dating back to a time before we'd met. He wanted to open it now and see what was inside, but he didn't have the combination and didn't remember if he had written it down or, if he had done so, then where that scrap of paper might be found.

Lacking a combination, and because Alan was living in a world of declining rational solutions, he wanted to employ his power drill to get inside, and he wanted to do it right now. Such a maneuver would be risky in the hands of a person with dementia. Think of a power drill held horizontally against a metal safe bolted to a concrete ledge. Think of the whirring drill bit glancing off the metal, striking concrete, slipping so the bit end runs wild. But the power drill project excited him. I was reminded once again that this was a man who still wanted his freedom, his independence, a former engineer who wanted to solve problems and triumph over inanimate objects.

Then I noticed a serial number on the safe. "Wait," I said, "let's contact the safe company and see if there's a way to get a copy of the combination. Maybe it's registered." With hope for a non-injurious solution, I wrote the number down.

But he still wanted to drill.

Resorting to the technique called redirection, I set about uncoupling the power drill fixation. Food often works, so I lured him out of the basement with a promise of one of my special tuna salad-egg-cilantro sandwiches. I closed the basement door. Next, to get us out of the house after lunch, I quickly ordered two online tickets for the three o'clock showing of the astronaut film, *The First Man*. The food and film worked, and he forgot about the power drill. My relief and gratitude for his forgetting was the upside of this terrible downside malady.

While he was eating his sandwich and repeatedly thanking me because he was always appreciative of my culinary efforts, I grabbed my laptop and checked the safe manufacturer's website. A dropdown menu item told me how to request a lost combination: I'd need three pieces of information, one being Alan's ID. I retrieved his old driver's license from where I'd stashed it, keyed in the number along with the purchaser's address and the serial number I'd found, then hit send. Yay, I thought, another problem solved. Except I promptly received an email declining my request.

Sentry had done an instant security check to find out if Alan was who he said he was and, yes, residing at this original address, but it came up that his driver's license was no longer valid. This stopped us from obtaining the combination until we took the step of obtaining his Senior ID. That was a wake-up call, for even if we had stopped traveling and he no longer did his own banking or shopping, sometimes he would still need his ID. Now we had to arrange for an appointment at the DMV.

On the designated day, I had to negotiate our departure step-by-step: Select clean clothing from the closet. Fight off distractions with "Okay ... maybe you could do that later?" Once he was clad in a neat pair of khakis, a belt, and clean, long-sleeved shirt, socks and with not slippers but street-worthy shoes on his feet (another hurdle), he headed to the closet to pick out a tie.

He loved his large collection of ties, and I loved the fact that he could still manage to select one then tie it, a good sign twice over. This was the last step in getting dressed and a sure ticket out the door. He picked out a tie with a design of little antique cars to wear to the DMV. We were almost on our way. Or so I thought.

What remained was negotiation about what kind of kit he would take along, his huge cluster of keys, for example. And then he reached for his multi tool, which had several nested knives. "There's likely to be a security check at the entrance to the DMV," I said, "so maybe you'd better leave the tool with the knives behind." Reluctantly he agreed, and finally we were out the door.

Once at the DMV, we learned that we could fill out a paper form, sure, but we were told that the best option to avoid a long delay was to use one of the available computer monitors. "No problem," my husband said because in times past he had been a whiz on computers.

I was standing next to him when he tried to key in his address. He froze. "I don't remember my address," he said. I reminded him, and he entered it. He next found that he had lost his ability to navigate the menu on an electronic device. I had to do it for him.

We finally completed the electronic form and then headed for the photo station, which brought an unexpectedly upbeat moment, for me at least. Alan was next up for having his photo taken, and behind him stood a short line of people. A thirty-something man turned around and said to me, "Your husband looks so dapper." Clearly Alan and I were an age-matched couple, the most senior in the place.

I felt proud of him. After so many battles lately over not showering, struggles over his trying to wear yard- or garage-dirty work clothes even if we were going out to a restaurant, it did my heart good to see him looking like his old self: tall, trim, professorial, still physically fit, a picture of dignity.

This turned out to be a special day in more ways than just superficial appearance. It was also an occasion for another epiphany. After we returned to the car, he shook his head as if in disbelief. "I forgot my address. I couldn't work the computer." He sighed. "That brought home the reality. I get it. I understand why I can no longer drive."

Maybe it was also the locale—the Department of Motor Vehicles, where he had renewed his license ever since moving to California in the early 1960s—that led him to this realization. Both technology and his mind had changed. There would be no going back to the way it once was.

How I Got Rid of His Guns

WE WERE HABITUAL viewers of the PBS News Hour, but it didn't matter which news source you watched on February 14, 2018, when a horrified nation learned that a student gunman had slaughtered seventeen people at the Marjory Stoneman Douglas High School in Parkland, Florida. Looping on the screen through multiple news cycles, the visual of those fleeing, frightened high school children was heartbreaking.

"Another sad reason for passing gun legislation," said Alan, being outwardly against gun ownership. But I knew he owned handguns because he had mentioned them in his more lucid days. I hadn't actually seen the guns in our two decades of marriage, but I knew they lurked somewhere in the house.

Moreover, like the young shooter in the Parkland tragedy— and like the other madmen who slaughtered innocent people in churches and schools and their colleagues in a workplace and festival goers in Las Vegas—the man sitting next to me also had a type of mental illness. In this case, his was an as-yet unspecified but progressive form of dementia, even though, in the second month of 2018, it seemed in an early stage.

According to a 2017 Pew Research Center Study, about half of people over age 65 have guns in their households. Factor in the nine percent of Americans 65 and older who are diagnosed with dementia, and the intersection can be deadly. I have read about cases of men with dementia who shot their wives after mistaking

them for strangers. But in early 2018, my husband was still articulate and mainly rational, not someone who would mistake me
for an intruder. Or could he? I knew from the accounts I'd heard
at my support group that, chances are, some day he won't recognize me. It could be months or years, but it would come.

The terrible Parkland incident gave me an idea, so I decided to seize the moment. "Our anniversary is tomorrow," I said.
"As a couple, I would like us to do something important. I know
you believe in gun control, so let's show our solidarity with these
young people and get rid of your guns."

"Do you mean … sell them?"

The tone indicated he wasn't thrilled. It is hard to separate
a man from his tools or his guns, even a man who doesn't believe
in owning the latter in the first place.

"I suppose so," I replied. At that moment, I didn't consider
other options.

"There are two guns," he said, "and they are quite valuable.
I inherited them from my uncle. I don't have permits, making it
more complicated."

"Complicated, that's for sure," I said. I wasn't about to
suggest trying an illegal sale. I thought I had hit a wall, and so
months passed as I deferred finding a solution to this problem.

For the past several months, driving had been my main focus at
the Alzheimer's support group, but by fall of 2018 that had been
resolved. Now I brought up my gun concern with the support
group. We discussed another option apart from selling, and that
was turning them in to the police.

Before I called the local precinct, I pictured myself carrying them in, say, inside a sealed brown box. But no, I was told a squad car would come by. The officer spoke firmly. "Leave the guns exactly where they are, whether in a drawer or somewhere else, until we arrive." It sounded like a command. My phone call had begun the procedure for removal, which would take place later that day.

I told Alan that I'd merely begun research when, inadvertently, I had initiated a process, and knowing his guns did not have permits he couldn't stop what was now in motion. I threw in a fib when I said, "I'm sorry." Or maybe it wasn't entirely a fib but an acknowledgment that this step would strip away another thread of his identity, one dating back to his army days because he appreciated weaponry despite believing in limits on ownership. And maybe because of this, he didn't hear me when I added, "I was told by the officer not to touch the guns. He said to leave them exactly where they are."

A black-and-white was scheduled to park at our curb within in a couple of hours. I thought this might seem alarming to residents on our quiet, leafy street, so I decided to alert the neighbors on both sides ... and also to take this occasion to inform them about Alan's condition. This elicited sympathy, and I learned that my neighbor to the north had lost her father to Alzheimer's not long ago. Telling them about our situation was a positive step for another reason, too. In the future when I needed help, they would be there for me.

I began to prepare dinner in late afternoon, and when I came back into the dining room, I saw that he had retrieved the two handguns from their hiding places and set them, along with carry cases and ammunition, in a heap on the dining room table. "But the officer said not to move them!" I whined, now pointlessly, because there they were. It was done.

I went back into the kitchen, but then—from a room away—I heard a gunshot. *Oh my god!* I ran back into the dining room, nearly frozen with the fear he'd chosen suicide. But there he stood, unharmed, a bewildered look on his face. "It went off," he said vaguely. The room still smelled like cordite, and there was a bullet in the wall.

"Please, please, don't touch them again."

"No, I won't." He sounded sheepish. "That was an accident."

The police came about an hour later. I wondered if they could smell the recently fired weapon, sense something was amiss, but they didn't mention it. They asked about the history of the guns and filled out a form, which Alan signed. When they left with the two guns, one officer left a card and said, looking me squarely in the eye, "Call me if there is *anything* else."

Yes, there was, and it ate at me, so a few minutes after they left, I phoned his number. "I didn't mention it," I said, "but my husband accidentally fired one of the guns. It happened maybe an hour or so before you came."

"What did it hit?"

"The wall in that same room."

"Is the bullet still there?"

"Yes, it is," I said.

"We're coming back."

It was dark when the black-and-white pulled up to the curb again. I showed them the hole, and that seemed to close the case. I was relieved.

The guns were gone, the misfire hadn't been aimed at himself, or at me, and I slept like a stone that night.

One Dream Dies, Another Takes Flight

MAYBE ALAN HAD a time-to-stop-driving epiphany at the Department of Motor Vehicles, but that hadn't stopped him from pursuing another form of independent transportation. On DMV day I didn't know this surrogate was already in transit, on its way—the rechargeable electric tricycle or E-Trike he had ordered online, weeks ago.

Such rechargeable devices would become popular here a few years later, but they were rare, mostly for commercial use, and still novel at the time. This one, made in China, was a heavy duty model used for deliveries. It had both manual pedal power and electric power, and for the latter, an upper speed of about 25 mph and ten miles higher if you pushed it. It did not require a license and was not legal on a highway.

What we soon came to simply call the Trike arrived in a large box. Once he'd opened it, with me hovering nearby, Alan recognized that the kit needed professional assembly.

I gained a kind of deferment while we waited for an appointment with a busy technician, who was solidly booked ahead for weeks. I wished the delay could last forever. Eventually, though, a tech from the distributor made a house call and soon the Trike was up and running. I had grudgingly accepted that it was here to stay.

He had agreed to a few safety rules: Only ride the Trike on the streets of our neighborhood. Not drive it on the hazardous 30-mile-long Santa Ana River trail, which has an access ramp near our house. Tell me if he was going to take it out on a run. I took a deep breath and added, "I will keep the two keys on my key ring."

Indignant, he reminded me that he had made nearly 500 skydives and participated in risk sports like Scuba for decades. "Yet now," he yelled, "now I am not even allowed to have a key to my own Trike?"

"But this is different," I replied, fighting back the urge to explain with rational points, points he would surely reject about the dangers involved with his affliction: his demonstrably failing judgment, his warped sense of perception, and his sketchy peripheral vision. Anger or no, the upshot of this was a tag on our key rack that said Ask Allene for Trike key. And these keys could not be duplicated.

He asked for the key a few times, took short rides, and brought it back. Then one Sunday I looked outside and noticed that both Alan and the Trike were gone. No note. At first, I wasn't too alarmed. I'd been under the impression that I controlled the only keys, without which he would be limited to manual, meaning pedal power. I doubted if he'd ride it more than a couple of blocks in the neighborhood because with the heavy Trike purely on the pedal setting it would be slow going.

When he reappeared, I stopped worrying, that is, until later that night when we were watching TV and he yelped out in pain.

"What's wrong?" I asked. "Where does it hurt? Do we need to go to the ER?" I was in a panic.

"No." He winced. "It's nothing to worry about ..." But soon he cried out again.

"My God—what is it?"

"Okay, here's what happened," he began, sounding chastened. "I was riding it in the neighborhood. I had an accident."

"What?"

"I lost control and fell backward into the mechanism, onto the handlebars or maybe onto the battery or something, and I hurt myself ... here." He pointed at his scapula, or shoulder blade, the wings at the backs of the shoulders.

"Oh, let me see," I said. We pulled up his T-shirt but I saw no break in the skin. When I touched where he had indicated before, he let out another cry.

"We'll call the orthopedist first thing tomorrow."

Fortunately, the doctor had a cancellation and we were scheduled for mid-morning.

Sitting in the office, I watched as the doctor probed and asked what had happened. Alan replied with an engineer's precision: "I was riding my electric tricycle. It's an electric, pedal-assisted model. As I headed down the ramp on the river trail, which is actually a flood control channel, I lost control and fell sideways on the trail and hit the mechanism. I probably landed against the handlebars."

On the 30-mile river trail—but he'd agreed not to go there! I pictured the steeply angled sides of the concrete embankment. What if he'd fallen the other way? Toward the steep drop-off? And he'd been under electric power, after all. Only later on would I figure out that he had quietly wangled an extra key during the assembly visit by the technician.

The doctor diagnosed the problem as an ordinary injury, requiring nothing more than over-the-counter pain relief. We left the doctor's office with Alan still wincing and me steaming about his hazardous adventure. I was trying to wrap my head around why this had happened. Why had all rules been scuttled? Here's the answer: because he was in survival mode and was seizing on any strategy that might extend his independence. This maneuver, however, had had the opposite effect.

As soon as we got home, I turned to him. "This could have been so much worse because you could have fallen down the embankment. Why can't you just do what we'd agreed and stay on the streets of our neighborhood?"

"Because I don't want to. Those streets are no challenge."

I waited a beat. "Then I think we should sell the Trike."

I expected a fight, but he just sighed. I was astonished when, as during his epiphany at the DMV, he said, "I know. I get it. The Trike didn't work out as I'd hoped."

Now It is April 11, 2019, and if I am lucky and all goes well, the Trike will be sold today.

I had nightmares last night. In one, I dreamt that the three-wheeled monster and ongoing source of conflict between us would be stuck here forever. Or was this stuck-here-Trike dream a stand-in for this disease of unknown duration?

We were both up early. At first, I didn't notice that he'd headed into the garage. I checked as soon as I could and found him with a wrench in his hand, tinkering with the basket attached to the Trike's handlebars. Was he taking it apart so the buyer would reject it?

Trying not to sound too concerned, I asked, "Um ... what are you doing?"

"Tightening screws. Some of them seem loose."

I flashed on the irony of his remark, though it was not an occasion to smile.

"I guess I'd just leave it as-is," I said, trying to sound casual. "If the buyer wants them tighter, he can do it himself. He said on the phone he's a motorcycle instructor, so I'm sure he has the right tools."

Alan set down the wrench and no longer seemed hell-bent on wreaking damage on the vehicle after all. He didn't seem angry, just sad. Maybe it was simply a last chance to curry his horse, stroke his pet, while he could still call it his own. For most of the next hour, he stood near it, changing position as if memorizing it from all angles.

Eventually, he looked up and voiced his original plan, about which I'd had no idea. "I thought I could take it up the river trail and teach." So it hadn't been a rogue action, it wasn't arbitrary after all. He told me he'd planned to take it ten miles up the embankment trail to California State University, Fullerton, as if he hadn't retired three years earlier, as if he would resume his role as a professor, presenting math lectures, holding office hours, then take the Trike along the river trail home.

Maybe it had been a secret dream that kept him going since losing his driver's license. Having different wheels. Teaching again. I wanted to distract him from his losses. "Let's go to a film this afternoon," I said. "Afterward, we'll have dinner at one of our favorite places."

"Okay," Alan said, his voice flat with dejection.

The buyer of the Trike, a wiry man named Randy, arrived promptly at 10 a.m. When I waylaid him at the end of the drive-way, I noticed he was wearing a T-shirt with a graphic of a wild man on a motorcycle. I mentioned to Randy that my husband had memory issues, a warning in case Alan said something odd, or if he resisted the sale. I made it clear that I would be the one handling the transaction.

We reached the garage, where Alan was standing, and I said, "This is Randy. He's a professional motorcycle instructor." They shook hands, and it seemed as if Randy's bold T-shirt and professional confidence caused Alan to perk right up. This buyer was not your average Craig's List shopper, but a pro. He knew what he was purchasing and how to handle it.

Alan pointed out the supposedly loose screws, and Randy said, "I'll probably remove the handlebars anyway." He explained that he was familiar with the electric vehicle—he already owned a two-wheeled version—and as they exchanged observations about the E-Trike and the pedal-assist design, I saw how Alan was lapping up the chance for the guy-talk so absent in his limited life with me. No matter what safety and comfort and distractions

I could give him, I couldn't give him the fundamental pleasure of relating to someone of his own gender, one of The Boys. If I silently lamented about how my life had become a trickle, his had turned into an arid savannah. I wondered if I could find a way to bring conversation with men back into his life.

At one point, Alan voiced something that caused a puzzled expression to appear on Randy's face. "The great thing was," my husband was saying, "I didn't need a driver's license to drive it on city streets." Randy and I glanced at each other. This had been Alan's last chance to drive a powered vehicle.

Randy, aware of the memory issue, smiled and said something diplomatic, then he pulled out a fat roll of cash. He handed it to me and said, "Go ahead and count it," which I did. It was the price we'd agreed on by phone. Alan didn't even ask how much was in the roll, and I think he didn't want to know. It was one fifth of what he'd paid less than a year ago.

Still, the transaction was going smoothly, and I could hardly believe my husband's good mood. We walked down the driveway with Randy as he rolled the Trike out to his pickup. He had a motorcycle-sized tow cart attached to the back, and now he attached an extension consisting of a pair of ramps. The three-wheeler rolled right up and into the carrier like a well-behaved filly. Randy shut the back gate and we shook hands all around, then we watched him drive away.

To my astonishment, my husband said softly, "I feel like a great weight has been lifted from my shoulders."

Who knew? But maybe my Alzheimer's coach had known all along. In one session, after I'd provided the support group with an earlier update on the saga of the Trike, I'd mentioned that for some reason Alan rarely took it out on the road, though I was glad it wasn't more often.

"Maybe he doesn't ride it more frequently because he's afraid," Audrey said. "Maybe he knows he might lose control."

And that was what had happened two weeks earlier, when he'd lost control. And that had led to today's sale, and now a new kind of closure.

Randy had barely pulled away and we had walked part-way back up the driveway when I saw that one of our butterflies had just emerged, or eclosed, from its chrysalis moments before. Its orange and black wings, still folded tight like a flower bud, glistened in the sun.

My gratitude on this bright day was now complete.

I was grateful for Randy, the perfect buyer. He gave Alan a sense of dignity by passing the Trike along to a professional.

I was grateful for the timing of this newbie butterfly, un-furling like a dream of flight. Now Alan and I moved in closer, our heads inches apart. We were in our best zone, where there is no strife, praising the creature and encouraging its effort with a kind of verbal duet. Up close now, we could see the gender indicator on the wing veins, and Alan said, "It's a beautiful and perfectly formed male."

For the next hour or so, we kept returning to the driveway to watch the monarch as it dried its wings to complete the last phase of metamorphosis. Among other things, we were making sure it didn't fall or get tangled in the shrubbery. The butterfly gradually stretched his wings to full span.

The four separate sections had fused, so at this point he was nearly ready to fly. Using the tiny claspers on the tips of his legs, he climbed to the top of the trellis, seeking the highest position. Once there, and after a final test of his wings, he gained lift and floated up into his new life.

Was it too much to hope that Alan felt some of that sense of freedom now that the Trike and its obvious dangers were behind him? Maybe he was consoled by the knowledge that we still have so many chances ahead to watch monarchs rise up, bank in a breeze, and soar away.

His troublesome boy-toy was gone, but he still had camera equipment, and it seemed there were limitless opportunities to collect images of our garden visitors. Photography had been a decades-long hobby for both of us. Twice we made winter trips to Death Valley and captured the desert's stark contours. Eventually, we each took home an honorable mention from a regional competition for our interpretations of the undulating sweep of sand dunes.

Compared to landscapes, chasing photo ops of insects may seem odd, but we were not alone. Many members of monarch Facebook groups—one approaching seventy-thousand members at the time I am writing this—post daily photographs of monarchs taken in their gardens, both stills and videos of the black and orange glow of butterflies, the antics of the yellow-and-black striped caterpillars.

In 2014, Alan and I had started a blog called Santa Ana Butterfly Garden, posting when we had images worthy to share.

I added captions, and often a photo came with a story. For the better part of those still-manageable-dementia years, it was common for a voice to carry through the open back door, "Quick, grab your camera!" and later, "Bring your iPhone!" Something dramatic and photogenic was happening outside.

Maybe it was a monarch emerging, or a female laying eggs, or a caterpillar gyrating from the J position and forming a chrysalis in seconds, before your eyes. Or it might be caterpillars engaging in curious or just plain weird behavior. Like a family album of sorts, we wanted to freeze such moments before nature's timetable moved on.

One day he called from the garden, "Come see this!" Maybe I sighed briefly if I was working on something, but when it came to drama in the garden, I didn't want to miss a thing. Soon I stood beside him but saw nothing unusual. It looked like a medium-sized, third stage caterpillar. Then he pointed. "Look closely." And I saw the difference. This caterpillar had rows of little diamond shapes between the usual lines encircling its body. "I just looked it up," he said, "It's a Queen."

The Queen, a rare visitor, is a near copy-cat of a monarch, and along with another look-alike, the Viceroy, make up what are known in the butterfly world as the Royal Court and all feast on milkweed. In their butterfly phase, their markings differ slightly. The Queen and Viceroy have extra black lines on their wings, like a slight variation in stained glass. We had never seen a Queen, now here was this fat little caterpillar, gorging away, oblivious to us taking its portrait.

It wasn't surprising that Alan spotted the visitor in our garden. Before his illness, and even in the early years, his approach to the butterflies was more scientific than mine. He savored the details and wanted to experiment with more unusual kinds of milkweed. Two species, less common at that time but native to our region, are narrow leaf and showy. He particularly wanted to succeed with the showy variety when he saw online images of its blossoms, so he ordered both kinds of seeds.

He had read that starting milkweed from a seed is more difficult than buying one already growing in a gallon pot, but this species wasn't available as seedlings from local garden suppliers. Planting these seeds is not the way it happens in nature, when at the end of a season pods appear, bursting with thousands of seeds that disperse in the wind. Some of those bring forth the next season's milkweed.

Despite Alan's careful efforts and watching for signs of green life in the soil almost daily, the narrow leaf and showy seeds failed to thrive. But no matter, we thought. We had plenty of the tropical species along the driveway, our prime area for sun, and in our back yard. It was perennial and thrived all year. Monarch butterflies flocked to it and their caterpillars seemed to love dining on tropical milkweed, the way little kids love cheeseburgers. We thought we were doing the best job possible to support our visiting monarchs.

We also perused monarch-themed websites. Some sold net enclosures for the so-called "rearing" of monarchs, a practice that would later become prohibited in our state. The enclosures, which come in various sizes, have one side that zips open and closed for access and one side of clear plastic for observation.

We owned one small collapsible net cube, though we did not intend to raise them. We had purchased it at the Natural History Museum shop in 2013, the day we were first inspired to undertake our butterfly adventure. Our purchase was part of a backyard kit intended for a child or a family activity. This small net enclosure later proved to be the perfect temporary shelter on a rare occasion when rescuing a monarch in trouble.

An intervention like that was legal at the time, as was captive rearing of monarchs in enclosures. We had no intention of practicing captive rearing because nature was doing fine in our back yard, along with an occasional light-touch of an assist, a minor rescue, from us.

Our net-enclosure purchase took place in 2013.

In the early phase of Alan's dementia, we made another trip to the Natural History Museum.

We'd received an e-mail announcing a Nature Garden event, so when that date dawned bright and clear, off we went. Our NHM membership benefits included admission to the Butterfly Pavilion and the popular Annual Bug Fair (always a sell-out), as well as this upcoming Nature Garden event.

After parking, we walked between the pillars of the classical façade and into the main museum building, past the skeletal brontosaurus, then down a decades-worn marble staircase. Once on the outdoor lower level, we followed a walkway lined with booths representing native plant restoration and other conservation organizations. There were a few whose mission concerned wildlife, one featuring a docile horned owl, dozing.

This was an outing on a beautiful day, with our planned patio lunch at the NHM café. Alan, being a sponge for science-based details, hoped to hear a few tips to elevate our monarch project. We'd walked in with milkweed on our minds.

I'd say we were primed to brag a bit about our success, which was based on the several dozen plants that had served as hosts for a hundred or more caterpillars that had developed into healthy monarchs. We believed we were doing our part to help a vulnerable species thrive.

At one booth we saw an array of blossoming native nectar plants: Buddleia, Salvia, Yarrow and others. I mentioned that we were monarch gardeners and the woman behind the counter responded with, "Then you know nectar plants are important as food for supporting all pollinators, from hummingbirds to bees and butterflies.

"I understand," I said, "we alternate milkweed with blossoming nectar plants." She nodded approvingly.

After we'd sauntered past a couple more booths, we came upon another native plant organization, native being relative to a region. Monarch gardeners in other states, of course, have different native milkweed in their gardens.

I blurted out something like, "Hi, my husband and I are monarch gardeners."

"I have to ask ..." she said warily, "what kind of milkweed do you grow?" The woman had the piercing look of an inquisitor.

"Well," I replied, "the kind with red and yellow blossoms."

"Tropical." Alan fired off the scientific name, *Asclepias cur-*

rassavica. She shook her head and I sensed bad news coming.

"If you call yourselves monarch gardeners then I think you should know better."

Ouch—what had we done? While we stood humbled like penitents, she held forth on why tropical milkweed is unhealthy for monarchs, how it is not native to California, or to the United States. Her lecture felt like a gut punch.

Okay, we knew about the relationship between milkweed toxins and monarchs. Toxins, when ingested in the right amount, protect the monarch from predators. This is responsible for the color of the caterpillars and butterflies, which signals to predators like birds that the animal is poisonous—Do not bite!

"Tropical milkweeed, being a year-round plant," she explained, "becomes too toxic. When caterpillars eat those leaves they can become sick. The condition, known as OE, short for *ophryocystis elektroscirrha,* can lead to deformed monarchs. When they mate, it impacts the gene pool."

So now we learned that not only did we have the wrong kind of milkweed but lots of the wrong kind of milkweed, though this was the only kind we'd seen for sale in nurseries in recent years. A year-round plant? We'd thought this feature was a plus. More food for monarchs. And it has pretty blossoms.

Back to our unforgiving critic at the native plant booth. "In this region you should grow narrow leaf or maybe the showy variety," she said, pointing to an example of narrow leaf. To me, the foliage of the aptly named narrow leaf looked so spindly that I failed to imagine a fat caterpillar balancing on such a flimsy leaf. The now-disgraced tropical plant had sturdy leaves.

"I tried both from seed," Alan said, "but they didn't thrive."

"Maybe you could try again." She softened a bit. "I know it can be difficult to start native milkweed from seed. You could try stratification, a technique that begins with seeds in the refrigerator to simulate a cold winter. You can look it up online. Or you could start with a seedling." She pointed to one. "Native milkweed dies back in the fall, then you ignore them over the winter. In spring, most of them rebound."

This was information we needed, but it was a downer. I wasn't ready to give up—what, rip out?—our thriving garden with its bright red and yellow blossoms. End visits from all the butterflies it attracts? It had supported so many new lives, and almost all I'd seen emerge from the chrysalis phase looked healthy. Maybe we'll lose a few to this disease, I thought, but sheer numbers must count. We're talking about helping a species in decline.

As we walked away from her booth, as if reading my mind, the woman called out an afterthought: "Until you manage to replace your milkweed with native varieties, at least cut the tropical plants close to the ground in October. Do it for the health of the butterflies. Do it for the future of their migration."

We were chastened that day, and unaware that within a few years this would become a campaign among the expanding number of monarch gardeners. A turning point came when the largest garden center in Southern California, Roger's Gardens of Costa Mesa, began offering a trade-in with this offer: Bring in a tropical milkweed ripped up from your home garden and we'll exchange it for a gallon-size pot of the native narrow-leaf species, free.

Chapter 3
BAH, WHO NEEDS HELP?

The Conundrums of Caregiving

I GUESS I'M BEING REDUNDANT, but here it is again. One of the most basic Alzheimer's Association rules for a family caregiver is this: If you do not take care of yourself, you cannot take care of your loved one.

Cathy kept urging me to seek assistance, and I kept reassuring her that our life was still manageable. I was doing fine. Her dad wasn't an invalid. We never went anywhere unless I could keep a close eye on him. And what would a day with home help even look like? This wasn't, after all, about someone helping with cooking or housecleaning. I could handle that on my own.

Plus, my husband stayed active around the house, puttering in the garage and pruning in the garden. Okay, yes, he was getting confused, and in the course of some of his projects he faced hazards, like potential falls. But I was home if he needed me, which on occasion he did. We'd ended up at urgent care for bruises, cuts and contusions a couple of times.

Truth was, if I did arrange for caregiving help, for someone to help me keep an eye on him, Alan would be irate, and I could just hear it: "Who is this person? I don't want some stranger hanging around me and loitering around my house!"

I was stalled at the prospect of Alan being constantly angry.

Yet I harbored my own resentments. There had already been incidents when his behavior threatened to ruin some of my personal connections. Years ago, I'd learned that writing isn't such a lonely craft if you befriend other writers. For two decades, I had organized monthly programs of speakers for my writer's organization. Even after Alan's dementia became apparent, I had been able to attend my monthly Saturday afternoon meetings because he'd been willing to come along, and then afterward he and I would go out for dinner. (There was my treat-as-bribe again.)

So far, it had worked out. During my meetings in the library community room, he'd spend those two hours reading one of his books in the other part of the library. I was glad that reading still engaged him.

Then there was an incident. No, make that two, and they shared a common theme. As he lost his independence piece by piece, he looked for new opportunities to say no, to push back. His job became resistance.

The first time it happened, he already had some driving restrictions but still had a license, and I still had my little red car. That day at my meeting, I was scheduled to introduce the speaker and manage the digital projector for her PowerPoint presentation, and

I also wanted to chat afterward with some of my writer friends. But when we reached the library, Alan said, "I don't want to go inside the library. I'll read in the car, so I'll need the key."

Not an unreasonable request; it made sense in a way. My Honda had power windows and it was a warm day, so, yes, he'd need the key to lower the window, catch a breeze, and not roast in the car. Not long ago he had agreed not to drive on freeways, and today he agreed not to use my car during my meeting. It had a conventional key rather than an electronic lock. I reluctantly handed him the key.

The community room had an exit with a little window overlooking the parking lot. Before the program began, I checked a couple of times and was reassured to see him reading or dozing in my car. After the meeting ended, two hours later, I cut short my social time and walked back to the parking lot and asked for the key so I could drive us to the promised restaurant. I waited while he turned out his pockets. Not there.

"Okay." I sighed. "Let's do a search." We emptied the glove box, probed under the seats and inside the cup holders, poked into crevices where it might have become lodged, but nada. The parking lot abutted a city park with an expanse of grass and trees and a small artificial lake. "Did you, by chance, take a walk in the park?" I asked.

"I don't remember. I might have," he replied, meaning the key could be almost anywhere.

Then I remembered that we had an emergency key in a small metal box hidden under the rear license plate. This was the first time we'd ever had to use it. I loosened attaching screws by using a dime, pulled off the plate and set it on the black surface of the parking lot next to my purse and tote bag full of materials. With things strewn around the car, it looked like a camping site.

As people filtered out from the meeting after the social hour, some of them asked, "Is everything okay?"

"No problem," I chirped. "Everything's fine." I was, of course, aware that lying had become my default position too often these days. Eventually, I had the extra key in hand and fired up the car. We were on our way to dinner at a steak restaurant with good memories for him, because, as he told it, years ago he'd once enjoyed a dinner here with his dad when he came to town on business. Once we got there, Alan was in a good mood. He eagerly devoured his steak, something he otherwise rarely ate, and sipped a glass of hearty red.

We never would find the lost key.

I knew that day the proverbial shoe had dropped. Alan's unpredictable behavior might end the writers club volunteer work that for two decades had formed an important part of my life and provided a source of many friendships. It was part of my identity.

What would happen next time? Could others still count on me? The answer turned out to be no, because the day of the next writers' organization meeting—when he and I were dressed, he had a book in hand, and we were ready to walk out the door—he balked. "I won't go," he said. "I'm not a dog on a leash." I couldn't leave without him, so I picked up the phone and found another member who'd take over my role at the meeting that day.

It was clear I could no longer make outside commitments. That is, not unless I hired home help. And that couldn't happen until I got past my angst about Alan's future rejection of strangers in the house.

Enter Cathy and her no-nonsense, intuitive way of approaching a problem, even at a time when she was raising a pair of teenagers. Here are a few lines from one of her emails:

> … *it's ok if my dad grumbles, yells, complains, and whines. I am firmly of the opinion that you need to be ok with this for a care-giving situation to start. Because – ultimately, we both know that a caregiver is needed for both his sake and yours. While he can't comprehend it now, before his mental decline, he would definitely not want you to sacrifice your well-being for him. You need to live your life. He would want that.*

It had taken me many months to finally get it through my head: The resilience of a caregiver spouse relies on holding on to the thread of her personal identity, of who she is. Of who I am. Now I had to find a way to take action.

Though grateful for the antics of each caterpillar, the green-and-gold beauty of a chrysalis, and the fluttering magic of the winged adults, monarchs weren't enough. Not enough to refresh, reboot, sustain the tolerance essential for my sanity. Every time I lost my patience, I felt overwhelmed by guilt: I would survive this fraught period of time, and he would not.

I needed a technique for fencing off the scary world of dementia unfolding around us, the fragments of unpredictability, the little shocks. I sought a feeling of flow. I needed to nourish the resilience a caregiver requires. Maybe a more disciplined person would meditate, but I knew from experience that my mind would be generating anxiety in a constant state of spin.

So, I looked at the given in a new way. Most days I could count on Alan being outside, working on trees or bushes or flowering plants, or puttering in the garage, though he would constantly shuttle back and forth, in and out of the house. He would patter into my office and interrupt if I was trying to concentrate on my desktop computer, or amble into the living room if I was reading and strike up a sub-rational conversation that, from my end—trying to follow the rules by not arguing, challenging, or reacting—was like verbally navigating a mine field.

Exhausting.

To bounce back and keep my love alive and carry on, I needed to find an indoor counterpart for our immersive visits to the monarch garden.

One space he always left off his walking itinerary of loops through the house was the guest room. This spot had potential, with a sofa that converted to a bed, comfy for reading a book with feet up, back propped against a cushion. It had two east-facing windows so I could check on his whereabouts, one close to the garage, the other overlooking most of the back garden. This could be my haven.

Books had often saved me in the zig-zag course of my life. Several retail bookstore positions since college, one providing a bridge to a decade in New York and a magazine editorial career. A bookstore management position came to the rescue when it was essential that I return to California to care for my mother. I'd trusted books to carry me forward and back like a flying carpet.

I made a little sign and hung it on the door: Reading. Please do not disturb. I hoped that with Alan's deep respect for books, these words would somehow get through to him. And it worked, surprisingly, for quite a while. Then I found a further workaround.

I've been told that I overuse the term workaround, but it often fits my condition at the moment. The word was coined in 1961 by someone in the computer community. According to Merriam-Webster, it is defined as: "A plan or method to circumvent a problem without eliminating it." Without eliminating the problem. You could say that by detouring around hurdles I had so-far avoided hiring home help.

In order to see my friends, now that Alan's behavior made that nearly impossible, I created a home Tea Room. I came up with the idea one Sunday when I felt like I was a captive in a scene from the movie *Groundhog Day*. I'll explain with a few notes from my journal that day:

> *I want to scream. Escape! I want respite from a repeating voice asking every few minutes, "Do we have a dictionary?" when there it sits, in front of him. I want to flee from his looping request to help him find an opinion show host he is obsessed with, but this is a Sunday and weekends she is not on the air. That fact doesn't dissuade him, so I find an old show and though her news commentary is weeks out of date, he thinks he is watching it for the very first time.*

Clearly, I was failing the caregiver's patience test and fed up with servicing repeated requests. Okay, fine, I decided. He can dwell in Groundhog Day if he wants to, but not me. I will flee. I said aloud, "I'm going into the guest room to read a book."

It happens that in the guest room we have a charming maple desk which has a drop front for writing and cubbies for letters, and above the writing surface are three tiered shelves. The desk dates to his boyhood, and I've always been fond of it. The upper shelves display our Chinese Yixing teapots, a collection we began when we purchased the first one in 1997 at a Chinese antiques store in Laguna Beach during our honeymoon weekend.

Now it was a different weekend, twenty or so years later. After I'd grabbed a book and curled up on the sofa, I looked across the room at the Yixing collection on the shelves and it came to me ... I would rename this space My Tea Room. Not only could I escape here alone to read, but there was enough space to set up a table and chairs.

I could invite friends into this space, set apart from whatever Alan happened to be doing somewhere in the rest of the house.

So I renamed it. And it's funny when you rename something for a different purpose, because the name can become prophetic. Not only would I invite friends for tea (now that it had become almost impossible for me to go to them), but another use soon arose.

For the past several years, I had attended a Monday night writers' group where five of us critiqued each other's work. I had stopped attending months ago because leaving Alan alone for almost three hours at night was too great a risk. Now I had a designated place to host the writing group, so I made the offer, and soon we began meeting on Monday nights at my house in the Tea Room. It felt like this change of role for a few square feet of the house enabled me to recapture a lost part of my life.

Except the larger problem of needing help with caregiving for Alan had not gone away.

Lessons From A Fever Spike

OVER THE YEARS, I'd been wiped out annually by a late-winter flu, but the bout in early 2019 was the worst I'd endured in a decade. I had no idea that exactly a year later, the nation would be plunged into the Covid 19 pandemic.

Though I had simply planned to tough this one out—sleep, sip soup, drink juice, lay low, repeat—there came a Saturday when my fever reached 103. And it hit me: if this turns into pneumonia and I land in the hospital, what will happen to my husband? He would be left home alone.

I pictured possible consequences: He decides on a whim to walk to the hardware store five miles away, leaves his iPhone behind or takes it along but the battery runs out. What if he becomes disoriented? What if he gets lost? A stranger might ask, "Are you all right?" and Alan might admit he needs help and pull out the Medic Alert ID medallion with contact information on a chain around his neck … and then again, he might forget he has that medallion. Dire possibilities surged in my feverish head.

Fortunately for me and for us, I dodged pneumonia that time, but the scare convinced me that I must immediately take the steps to arrange for a home caregiver. As soon as I was past the worst of the virus, which included losing my voice for a week, I called a private caregiver who had been recommended months ago, only to hear that he had just taken on a new full-time client.

I didn't need full-time help, anyway, just a few hours a week. I needed flexibility, so I began reviewing agency contracts for different home care services, learning such things as the minimum number of hours in a shift, which at that time turned out to be four. I was making progress toward keeping my husband safe in case of an emergency, if something should happen to me. And if I could cover sufficient hours so that I could reclaim some of my personal life too, that would be more than frosting on the proverbial cake. It would be essential for my sanity.

Though Alan still seemed capable of managing at home, he increasingly showed signs of bad judgment. He called it "optimizing" if he tackled an unnecessary home repair job then wrecked something, like plumbing. Pop, another crisis. Such actions made it more important that he not be left alone, that someone keep a discreet but watchful eye on him. That person, preferably male, would be my ideal caregiver. It was time to make that happen.

After I had looked into several home care agencies that didn't feel quite right, or maybe I was hampered by confusion, I tried a different approach. I had learned that one memory care facility also had a home care division. Westwinds, I'll call it, had a good reputation, and one of its locations was a ten-minute drive from our home. When I had a chance to briefly stop by, I saw that it had a welcoming atmosphere with big trees and three secured courtyards and friendly therapy animals. I thought Westwinds might be a good candidate should Alan, at some far future date, require memory care placement.

I could already see that for us to consider what is called a three-tier facility—a residential model where we would start in an independent apartment, then move to the assisted level, then Alan would move into memory care—was unlikely. This was because of the fast rate at which his dementia was progressing, not to mention that I felt far from ready for such a lifestyle myself.

The Westwinds company, which had a chain of memory care locations, not only had a home care division with caregivers specially trained for dementia patients, but it also offered another advantage: if we later chose Westwinds, some of the caregivers there would already be familiar to Alan and vice versa, surely helpful at a time of transition.

Transition, like placement, was another new term for me, both similarly loaded with guilt. The very thought of my husband transitioning into a memory care facility for placement, never to come home again, was far more distressing than anticipating his outrage over my hiring occasional caregiving help.

So I made an arrangement with the memory care facility to provide certified home care assistance. This meant paperwork and setting up an account. I specified that the helper be male, hoping that Alan, lacking male company and so highly cognitive, might have a chance to engage in conversation. Trained specifically for dementia care, this person would start by staying with my husband for one stretch of four hours each week, and I would thus gain a free afternoon and maybe book an overdue visit to the hair salon or catch up on one of my deferred dentist or doctor appointments.

But the home care arrangement required an initial assessment, which meant a coordinator had to meet both of us and conduct a home analysis. An appointment was set for a Tuesday afternoon at our house.

I guess I tried an ambush, maybe not the best idea, but I waited until almost the last minute, and then I chattered away to Alan about how I was hiring an assistant for me. He didn't buy it. He figured out that this meant a caregiver for him. He hated the idea. "I don't need a babysitter!"

Soon after we'd finished a silent lunch, a coordinator named Jaden arrived. She was a pleasant and attractive young woman, and that helped, I think, as far as my husband was concerned. When the two of them met, he was cool but civil, and after a handshake and a few brief words, he excused himself and returned to the back yard to resume his fruit-tree pruning.

She and I talked further, and I answered more detailed questions and signed the necessary forms. The meeting ended and Jaden drove away. When I checked on Alan, letting him know she was gone, he silently continued his gardening. So far, it had been a day fraught with tension, and I felt exhausted, so I decided to lie down for a short nap.

But I napped longer than planned, forgetting to set my usual 10-minute timer, and when I woke about an hour later, I went into the back yard. No one was there. I called his name. I checked the Man Cave, his garage workshop, and the front patio where he sometimes clips the Concord grape vine. I checked the north side of the house, where the camellia bushes grow.

No Alan.

He had never walked away before, never wandered, if that's what this was. *Aha*, I thought, it is obviously some kind of rebellion against my hiring home care assistance. Clearly, he is pissed off, but where could he be?

I clicked the Find My Friend app that I'd discretely set up on our iPhones and found his location. There was the slowly moving marker indicating that my husband was about ten blocks south of our home. I looked again and realized this meant he was near the civic center, where he had worked for three decades as a county civil engineer before he retired from that and took up teaching.

Resolved to keep my tone calm, I called, "Hi, Alan. Just wondering where you are." I said this as if his wandering away from the house and not telling me was an everyday occurrence.

"I'm on my way to the credit union to take out some cash."

"Oh ... okay," I said. "So I guess I'll see you afterward?"

"Sure," he said, but his tone was so clipped and dismissive that I wondered what he didn't say. What else was he planning?

Wild possibilities flashed through my brain. Was this a junket to take out cash and maybe flee by cab to the airport? If so, it would have to be by cab, because he didn't have a ride hailing service on his phone as I did. He had his senior ID, which would qualify for security on a domestic flight, but he no longer carried a debit card or a credit card, because by then I had hidden them, aka they'd been misplaced.

Could he withdraw a large amount of cash from our joint account if he had no debit card? In a surge of panic, I picked up the phone and asked to speak to a bank officer. Yes, she said in answer to my question, he could withdraw money with just his

Senior ID. It was perfectly legal. "But my husband has dementia," I said, sounding desperate. I waited a beat yet heard little reaction. "At least," I went on, "*at least,* would you take down my phone number and call me if anything goes wrong when my husband arrives at the bank?"

She agreed to write it down and call if a problem arose, but that implied that if there was no apparent problem then he could execute such a transaction. I considered driving to intercept him at the bank and no doubt cause a scene but decided instead to track Find My Friend and wait it out. I had noticed that he seemed to be walking in circles. About an hour later he showed up, entering through our back door.

"How did it go?" I asked, bland words compared to how anxious I felt.

"I've been to that bank hundreds of times and it's just a few blocks away from my old office," he said with the head toss of the clueless, "but I couldn't find the credit union. I got all turned around, walking those blocks."

"Oh, well," I began, figuring that the best strategy was not to mention how it seemed he had tried to punish me. "I'd say those hundreds of other times you probably went there by car. I guess any city looks different when you're traveling by foot."

Money Complicates Matters

I WAS SHOCKED by the realization that he might have tapped the bank account, taxied to the airport, and ended up ... who knows where, another looming cloud of this progressive disease.

As a couple who married later in life, we'd always filed individual taxes. Alan had a long-time accountant, I had mine. Then at some point in 2018, I had an ah-ha moment and became a suspicious wife, a financial sleuth, a sort of forensic accountant.

Had he ever filed his 2017 taxes? I poked around in his file drawer and saw no evidence, so I went behind his back and checked. "Well, no," said his accountant, "I left him a voice message, asking if he planned to file late. I called twice. I'm afraid there will be a penalty."

Clearly it was time for me to step into a new role. I was like a woman whose husband, the self-appointed manager of home finances, abruptly departs from this planet. Suddenly the task of sorting out money matters falls to the Surviving Spouse.

This role would take diplomacy, loving white lies, and redirection. I seized on opportunities when he was occupied elsewhere in the house. I poked around. Peeked in his check register. Saw that this man—who'd perfectly balanced his checkbook, and still did it manually—had stopped recording expenses more than a year ago.

I started pulling together documents, and for some items I requested replacements online. This turned into a Surviving

Spouse-lesson in the hurdles of access—locating passwords when your mate has dementia. I had once urged him to follow my system and note passwords on three-by-five file cards, now I partially reaped the benefit.

Tethered to our digital devices, it's clear that our nation is migrating to an online life with fewer printed bills landing in the mailbox. A few years back, Alan had set up automatic payments (EBT) for certain recurring monthly and other expenses. "More convenient," he'd said at the time, and mainly that was true. Except now I had to identify recurring debits when they appeared on his online checking or credit card statements, not least to spot anomalies in case of fraud.

A related complication arose. The company that issued his primary credit card replaced it for reasons of internal security, and the new card came with a different number—also with the annoying advice to notify automatic payees. Alan would have been bewildered, tackling this multi-step process alone.

I waited for the right moment then made an offer. "I'll be glad to serve as your secretary," I said, trying to act like a cheery assistant instead of a woman taking over the executive tasks he'd always handled so efficiently.

Of course, contacting accounts to change the card number not only requires a password, but in some cases it generates security verification via text or voice sent to his cell phone. Sometimes a live agent on the phone asked to speak directly to Alan for verification. Welcome to married life in an era of secure data silos, which may seem reassuring until you need to pry your way inside. And pry I did.

Alan's rogue stroll to the bank in 2019 was just the beginning of my dawning worry about how money could be misappropriated, captured by fraud, caused to evaporate. It also led to a banking trick I would need later on.

That day when he'd tried to access the bank in person, I was shocked to learn that with only an ID he could have walked up to the teller at the credit union and withdrawn enough cash to get away from home. Home was where he faced an increasing number of constraints on his freedom. That time his plan had failed because he became lost, but a block or two farther and he might have succeeded.

The bank walk-about was a sign of more incidents yet to come, a red flag warning telling me to ramp up my vigilance. What else could happen? I wondered. A lot, it turned out.

He was a math guy and still highly cognizant in this area, so I had to tread lightly. At the same time, he was losing his computer skills on his PC. He was losing his judgment. Losing the ability to connect cause and effect.

One day I passed by his home office and noticed he was on the telephone with his credit card in his hand. I heard Alan read off his card number. What I didn't hear was the first part of a conversation that had gone something like this: "So you will fix my software problem?" Someone on the other end of the line had said yes. My husband expected this fix would improve or restore his faltering ability to manage his PC. For this promise, he duly paid about two hundred dollars to "Microsoft," which was, of course, an impersonation, a scam. Plus, this impostor, who had solicited him by phone, now had his credit card information.

He was off the phone now, and I tried to explain what had just happened. First, we alerted the credit card issuer about the scam and were told we'd receive a new card. But the PC was part of the problem, like the car back when he was still driving.

I wondered Where else in the worldwide web will my husband go today?

Alan was a longtime PC user. My platform was a Mac. His daughter and I huddled in back-and-forth emails about his problem with the PC and decided to get rid of his old device so I could step in to help him ... especially if I needed to thwart him.

This technology swap turned out to be smoother than I'd expected. He resisted at first, but knowing his PC was an older model, or as he said, "giving him trouble," and knowing his wife and daughter were experienced Mac users, he gave in. That change was another step in the delicate dance of preserving my husband's dignity while delaying the inevitable loss of his independence.

Protecting him from himself while protecting me.

Then there was the overarching matter of banking. As someone who identified with his math skills, he would, from time to time, ask to see his online bank balance or the status of the investment portfolio. Typically, he couldn't figure out how to navigate the various financial online tabs and menus and he came to accept that I was his helper for online account navigation.

We would sit in front of his new Mac as I pulled up statements for him to view. He paid close attention, noticing totals and individual payments and withdrawals. "What was that payment for?" he might ask about an unfamiliar entry. I would interpret. When needed, justify.

Even as his dementia deepened, he would sometimes ask to see the bank balance and Fidelity account balance. These became obsessive requests, and I knew they were coming.

At one point, this routine would play a role in a critical expense. Flash forward to early 2020, when I would need to make a four-figure deposit for memory care, even though an admission date to the facility was still in the vague future. How would I explain that when Alan saw such a whopping item jump out in the bank statement?

His daughter and I huddled again. We decided on an indirect payment to her: I would employ another loving lie and tell him the withdrawal was for college costs. Instead, she would pay the memory care facility. When the day came and he noticed the item on the statement, I simply reminded him that it was for college tuition for the two grandchildren.

He nodded, sage-like, as if remembering.

Back to the *ah ha* moment that set me off on sleuthing. Eventually I had gathered enough material for a meeting to remedy the omitted 2017 tax filing. I made an appointment for the two of us and packed the items into a briefcase. Off we went. While we sat across from him, and I handed over paperwork, Hal, the accountant, cobbled it together.

Within a few days he had calculated what Alan owed, plus penalty, and we returned for Alan's signature.

"I can't believe," my husband said as he signed off, laughing sheepishly, "that I forgot to file my own taxes."

This was the new normal. I would be responsible for money matters from now on.

My Getaway with J.S. Bach

IT IS THE FIRST WEEK of May in 2019, and lately we've had a near-record number of caterpillars, as many as eighteen at one time, and a dozen successful chrysalides. We have surpassed nature's odds, as more than half of this cohort of caterpillars have succeeded in forming a chrysalis, each one an inverted pale green pear, decorated with a metallic gold band.

In other news, today marks my first getaway—a caregiver-covered, four-hour, Tuesday afternoon. Of course, Alan has been and still is dead set against having a home care person hanging around ever since he learned two weeks ago that such coverage had been arranged by me and for me.

I suppose I am anxious about our first caregiver's arrival, but he rings the front doorbell promptly at 1 p.m. and he makes a good impression. Carl is bright eyed, slim, maybe in his thirties, neatly dressed in civvies, no sign of medical garb other than a discreetly pinned-on badge. I introduce them, and when Alan is once again cool but civil, I am relieved.

The best news of all, though, is an unexpected icebreaker. Alan immediately takes Carl to the side garden and makes a kind of introduction between caregiver and caterpillars. He starts explaining about milkweed. Our amazing record of a dozen green chrysalides at one time gets my husband talking about all aspects of monarch lore. Carl, trained to engage a dementia patient, is a good listener. He shows respect.

But soon I have to interrupt Alan's monologue so I can show Carl to my Tea Room, where, in private, he and I exchange phone numbers for text messages, if needed. I assure him that he doesn't need to interact with my husband, if Alan seems unwilling. Carl mainly needs to look out through the windows—this room providing an ideal vantage point—and check on Alan, who will be working in the garden, most likely, or puttering in the garage, or maybe he will come inside and page through Facebook, if he can remember how. Above all, I say to Carl, "Don't let him walk away. It would be out of sheer rebellion, and not because he is disoriented, but because he is angry about having to tolerate the presence of a caregiver."

Once Carl is settled in the Tea Room, I get in the Toyota, now our only car, and pull around the corner, stopping at the curb under a tree. There I set up the car speaker on Bluetooth to play Pandora. Right away, I experience a rush of car-radio euphoria. Some years in the past, it might have been Cat Stevens or Elton John cranked up high, but today, I am in the mood for the crystalline notes of J.S. Bach.

Pulling away from the curb, I drive to my first errand. I never guessed how much I would relish the simple task of driving alone in a car, of cruising down familiar streets. It reminds me of when I first obtained my driver's license at age sixteen. The sense of freedom, of the world expanding. Look at me, I am queen of the road. It's a freedom that Alan, sadly, has lost.

My first stop is the Department of Motor Vehicles. I'll need to renew my license in the next two months, so I'm here to pick up the latest motorist's handbook, even though I know it's available online. I want the hard copy version so I can easily mark it up.

Brandenburg Concerto No. 3.

I increase the volume to nearly full blast.

On to my second errand—the Paper Depot—I deposit the recyclables: junk mail, catalogs, and magazines that Alan refuses to part with. He has become a hoarder since dementia took hold, which has turned me into a secondary hoarder because I've hidden these in bags in the back of my closet. If he saw this paper haul, should I toss it into our recycle bin, my covert action would be blown. Instead, in the past, I looked for chances to make a run to Paper Depot, but since I sold my car, the accumulation of paper has become massive. Today it's in the trunk, and from now on, I will have Tuesdays for all manner of getaway errands, including disposing of paper clutter like this.

French Suite No. 5 in G Major

Bach also accompanies me on my third errand to donate a few books to Friends of the Library.

Next up is The Art of the Fugue.

Hearing the complex structure of this music, it seems to be a metaphor for my complicated life of doctor's appointments, shopping, cooking, looking for lost objects, and (on an up note) caring for the caterpillars and sometimes squeezing in a bit of writing. I remind myself to be grateful for what I have, for what he and I still have together.

Ahh, a Bach cantata.

I'm recalling how when I was an undergrad at San Francisco State, I thirsted for the kind of music that was new to me then, jazz, baroque, classical. This stood in contrast to the pop music of my southern California high school days. Arriving in San Francisco in early 1964, I soon made the acquaintance of J.S. Bach at a coffee house called the Coffee Cantata.

Today, this medley of Bach on the Toyota's sound system conjures a college-away-from-home excitement more than half a century later. Swept away by nostalgia, I am stunned when, suddenly, sharply, I miss my husband.

We've been glued together and mainly at home for months now, the better part of two years, in fact, ever since the day in 2017 when his psychiatrist advised me to stop traveling. It hits me hard that I am experiencing a preview of the grief I'll feel when he is gone.

With Bach's help, I soon recover from the falling feeling of loss and carry on with my freedom drive.

I stop at a Starbucks for a latte, then I pick up a business card at an optician for an overdue eye exam I'll schedule for some Tuesday.

Suite for Solo Cello No. 1 in G Major

I end up at the local discount mall.

Shopping! It's been months, a year, because there's been no way for Alan to hang out while I peruse store displays, much less try on clothing. Surrounding myself with racks of fashion markdowns at the discount mall feels like another throwback, this time to my middle school days when I earned babysitting money and placed outfits on lay-away. It took patience.

Cutting into this second surge of recollection, I miss Alan again. Nostalgia seems to tap into my emotions like a recurring refrain.

Now I wonder, what is happening at home? No text from Carl means no apparent problems, but is Alan sulking and morose? Is the caregiver frustrated, rejected, not sure what to do with a client who doesn't want him there?

When I am inside the Neiman Marcus "Last Chance" store—a shop with high fashions I'd never buy, but I love exercising my reclaimed freedom to browse—I phone home, fearing I'll hear outrage.

"How's it going?"

"Fine," Alan says. "We're having tea and I've been telling him war stories about Berlin." I know he means war stories quite literally. He's been talking about his service with the U.S. Army during the hostile face down against the USSR that culminated in the building of the Berlin Wall.

By sheer coincidence, long-term memories for both of us are flowing into the present. Inspired by J.S. Bach on my first getaway Tuesday, my past is bubbling up. Funny, how some of our personal myths are surfacing on the same day, this landmark day, when I have taken a brave new direction after admitting, at long last, that I need home help.

Unfortunately, the first caregiver had a short tenure, only one week. I learned this when I heard he had left the company to accept another job. It seemed a shame, the coordinator said, after he and Alan had apparently enjoyed a congenial time together. The next Tuesday, a new care giver named Jerrod would arrive at the same time, 1 p.m.

That morning, Alan and I checked on the progress of a still-closed chrysalis that had attached itself to an air vent on the side of our house. When we bent down and peered inside the chrysalis, it became clear that when the newbie butterfly emerged, it would have trouble getting out.

We'd occasionally found pathetic remains when a caterpillar had inched its way inside a risky location for the fourth stage of butterfly transformation, but after emerging from its chrysalis either found its wings too large to get free, or the sides too slick to gain purchase in order to exit the space. But now that we had identified the problem, that would not be the fate of this monarch. Not if we could help it.

The sides of its chosen location were slick. "It will need to grip onto something so it can crawl out and gain elevation," I said. "Maybe we could guide it over to this lantana branch." The branch was maybe a foot away, and that twelve inches was a hazardous stretch for a newly emerged and tender butterfly. It might fall onto brick edging of the planter or into the shrubs. Such a fall could ruin the still wet and partially unfurled wings.

His cognitive ability and engineering chops largely intact, Alan walked into the garage and returned with a fat stick. He then took out his pocket tool and began sharpening the tip.

"What's that for?" I asked, being a bit wary because these days his projects were often counterproductive.

"I am making a bridge," he said.

A civil engineer, making a butterfly bridge. And, sure enough, he inserted one end of the stick into the ground under the destination lantana plant, and positioned the other end of the stick so it reached an inch or two into the vent and sat below the chrysalis. Now it would be possible for the butterfly, when it emerged (any minute now) to cross over the bricks and the gap and reach branches where it could safely dry its wings, then gain height for its launch.

I marveled at the varied and co-existing stages of Alan's affliction, at how embedded strengths sometimes rise to meet an occasion.

When Jerrod arrived at 1 p.m. that afternoon, a female had emerged from its chrysalis about two hours earlier. By now, its orange-patterned wings were set and seemed to be glowing in the sun. The usual introductions were made, and Alan pointed out how our latest butterfly had navigated over his bridge, climbed up the branch of the lantana bush, and was now at the highest point and ready for its maiden flight. As we approached, she fluttered her wings and, with the three of us watching, took off.

"How amazing!" Jerrod said as we all followed the monarch into the back yard, where it perched on the edge of the garage roof.

"What a show," he added as we walked inside so I could familiarize him with the Tea Room and its vantage point. A new butterfly was a dramatic way to welcome a new caregiver. I hoped it might be a good omen.

A few days later, I wake after a snooze alarm reboot, falling back into sleep as if seeking advice from the depths of my subconscious. My father claimed he discovered his best mechanical design solutions in dreams, recalled them upon the cusp of waking.

Maybe I could do this, too, if a sleep state is where my lifehacks or detours or workarounds live, waiting to be mined. One gleaning from this morning's snooze alarm was three words: silence and service. I interpret silence as just shut up when he baits me, spins a fabrication, defies common sense. When he rebels.

But what could service mean? I'm guessing it means do something. Bake cookies. Prepare a meal. Clean a floor. Keep on moving. Because purposeful action must be better than spinning my wheels. Maybe these catch words retrieved from sleep and repeated could help psyche me up, like an athlete facing the next physical challenge.

Mainly, I want to avoid losing it, as I did yesterday.

What was the trigger for my freak-out? Well, after trying two caregivers—and both seemed to have fit in quite well with butterflies and tea and stories and all—Alan refused to allow any stranger into our home, ever again. I exploded in outrage. How could he deny me four measly hours of coverage per week so I could get out and take care of personal business? My over-the-top angry reaction scared me, and I wondered, could blowing my top trigger a stroke? I have no pre-existing condition, but I wasn't so young anymore.

Anyway, when I was in this morning's snooze-alarm-consulting mode, the words came to me: silence and service. I thought, Oh, well, I'll try this, at least.

At the same time, I did not cancel the home care service as he'd demanded. Instead, I asked for a new helper, someone Alan had never seen before. Let's mix it up, I thought. Maybe Alan will forget about "no more strangers in our house." What I really hoped for was a caregiver Alan would tolerate, if not welcome.

When Tuesday rolled around a couple of days later, the agency sent Ryan. The monarchs once again played a welcoming role in his midday arrival. Alan was in the side garden when Ryan's car pulled up at the front curb. When he got out, I saw he was another nice looking, neatly dressed young man in his twenties. I waved to him and called out, "Just walk on back."

As we made our introductions in the driveway, and before Alan had time to muster a mistrustful vibe, I pointed out several pudgy yellow caterpillars next to where we were standing. Dangling from a trellis not two steps away was a green chrysalis. It sparkled in the sunlight.

"Wow, that is so cool," Ryan said about these temporary residents in our garden.

And that was only the beginning. It turned out that not only could Ryan engage Alan on many topics, but he also had a natural eye for this wildlife hobby of ours, and soon he was all in, making it his own. The first day he found two caterpillars we had overlooked.

In coming months, Ryan listened to Alan's stories. He became a crack monarch-spotter, often engaging in long outdoor sessions talking about them with Alan. He would routinely find caterpillars we'd missed and also locate hidden chrysalides. He'd take iPhone photos and videos of caterpillars and butterflies upon emerging, and in composition alone, many of his were better than ours. We would share photos with him via text messenger, even on days when he wasn't with us. Oh, and he'd hang out with Alan in the Man Cave and talk about tools, too.

But on that first Tuesday, I had only hope and a glimpse of promise. This caregiver Ryan looked like a keeper.

And he was.

Chapter 4
OUR FRIEND ROUTINE

Still, The Best of Times

WHEN ASKED ABOUT what one friend called "your world," I'd usually say, "We follow a routine and it's not so bad."

She meant how was I coping with Alan and the shrunken borders of our former life. I was reminding myself, repeatedly, that my reduced freedom counts for little in a world where bombs destroy cities and desperate migrants flee for their lives, where I am fortunate to have a comfortable home and sufficient means to solve many of these problems with Alan as they arise. The looming cost of future Alzheimer's care still lay ahead, but in the meantime, we were home-based and I intended to cope as best I could.

Routine is one of those ways.

For the last two years, heading to the fitness club on Mondays and Wednesdays has proved a stabilizing anchor in our week.

It gave Alan a sense of purpose because he would time and log his laps. It also worked off some of his frustration, and it kept him out of trouble for a few hours. And it gave me respite because I knew he was safely occupied. The gym manager on duty knew of Alan's condition and where to reach me, in another part of the gym and only a few steps away. It seemed perfect. Reliable motion.

Then, a month ago, we had to cancel our membership. I felt bereft, like another part of our life had been ripped away. Loss of routine meant more hours for days to go off the rails, more chances for the snares of conflicts we dementia caregivers are told to avoid. I missed it. I wanted the routine of our health club back!

But wait—I'm getting ahead of my story. What happened? Here's what went wrong and how I recovered what we'd lost, for while at least.

In his formerly athletic life, Alan had been devoted to long-distance running and competitive swimming, receiving awards in his youth as well as in master's competitions in middle age. Over the decades, I had dabbled in various activities, from aerobic dance to tai chi to rowing. When we signed up with the health club, I looked at the schedule and found an activity that appealed to me. I'd learn Pilates at the same time Alan was in an open swim session taking laps in the pool.

We next added on another pleasurable part of our routine. After our workout, we'd drive across the street to a large Albertsons grocery store. It had a Starbucks inside, where we'd start with a latte each and share a chocolate nut bar. Alan would wait for me at a little café table and scan through largely promotional messages on his phone while I sipped my latte, rolling a cart down the aisles and checking off my grocery list.

The Albertsons stop had another benefit. It enabled me to keep up with the unusual ingredients I might need for a non-athletic activity: trying out new recipes. This fit into my keep-busy-service idea because Alan was always appreciative of my cooking and generous with compliments, if perhaps a bit over the top. Sometimes he would say such things as, "Delicious!" and "I'd easily pay twenty dollars for this dish in a restaurant."

Because of our twice-weekly visits, the cashiers and managers came to know us and so did the Starbucks baristas. Albertsons became like a home away from home, and the touches of socialization were good for Alan, plus our routine stops fit together like feathers on a dovetail: From 9 a.m. to noon, we had a steady half day of gym and shopping on Mondays and Wednesdays.

Then Alan started having trouble in the locker room, which reflected his decreasing capacity for recognizing objects. It started with a towel, mistaking some else's towel for his. It could happen to anyone, right? He admitted that he had argued with the other man, but said the mix-up was quickly resolved. Then we had another stretch when everything went smoothly.

Logistics are central when you're living with someone with dementia, so when we first joined the health club I'd wondered what type of lock to buy to secure his personal items inside the locker in the men's dressing room. The idea of a key lock wouldn't work, because by now he was routinely losing almost everything. How would he manage a key? Pinned on each time? Pinned on to what? And so I bought a simple numeric lock, even though I was unsure if he could remember the combination.

He managed for a while, because we set it to his daughter's birthday. Then, one day a couple of weeks later, when I was sitting in the waiting area, having completed my Pilates class, Alan appeared in the lobby clad only in a towel. Imagine the startled looks of the other club members. He walked up to the desk, and I overheard him say he had forgotten the combination to his lock and needed someone to cut the lock off. Before I could intervene, he and the manager, with a bolt cutter in hand, had entered the men's locker room and were out of sight.

We will surely find a way around this so it won't happen again, I thought.

My next proposal was not using a lock at all. Once we were in the car after the incident in the lobby, I said, "Why don't you leave home wearing swim trunks under your jeans, then hang the gym bag with your street clothes on a hook by the pool? You can change in the locker room after your swim and keep your bag with you—no need for a locker or a lock."

"No," he said. "I have always used a lock in a gym. It's called a *locker* room."

I sighed. It is typical of a dementia patient to cling to lifelong habits, even if they no longer make sense.

His next comment should have been in the past tense because he had given up teaching a few years ago, but now he said, "Of course I can work a combination lock. I am a college math instructor." He paused, then added, "And I want to prove myself."

I sympathized. We were both struggling with a vanishing identity, and I wanted to help him succeed.

So we bought another numeric combination lock, and in my own gym bag I started carrying along paper slips printed with the combination. Service, I reminded myself. Obviously, I couldn't enter the men's locker room, so I told him, "If you have a problem with the lock, send someone to the lobby and I'll give him a printed copy of the combination."

I adapted by leaving my class early in order to be ready in the waiting area by the time Alan was changing. I knew the timing precisely because that's when open swim ended and a water aerobics class took over the pool.

Except when he forgot the new combination, he didn't seek my help. When he showed up in the lobby again wrapped in a towel, this time I scurried to the desk and handed the printed combination not to my husband but to the manager, who looked at it and sighed. Learning he was tapped for yet another lock rescue mission, he turned to Alan and said, "Buddy, how about next time you just hang your gym bag on a hook by the pool? No need for a lock."

I tried to suppress a smug smile. Naturally, Alan rejected this idea flat-out. But after we left the gym that morning, he agreed to try a lock with an alphabetical combination, though he grumbled that one with letters seemed childish. The problem was, this type required not three letters but four, so if we used his three initials then the last letter was arbitrary. We added a Z. Within a couple of weeks, of course, he forgot this and appeared in his towel again. This time I was ready in the lobby. I called out to him, "It ends in a Z," and he said, "Okay," and trotted back into the locker room.

My belief in the security of our routine was faltering. What would go wrong next time?

It turned out to be a spatial-perceptual problem typical of advancing dementia that fed into another symptom. Paranoia. One of the first signs of that was the day when he couldn't find his locker at all. His eyes just didn't register, could not focus on finding his usual locker or the distinctive alpha-style lock. Not finding these, he jumped to a conclusion: his belongings had been taken.

Cut to another towel-wrapped appearance in the gym lobby busy with club members in their workout gear. "My things have been stolen!" he proclaimed at top volume.

Perched on a padded chair nearby, I heard and immediately intervened. "It's okay, honey," I said. Turning to the manager, I said, "I'm sorry, but would you please have someone walk the locker room with my husband. I'm sure his things are there and he just can't find them. His lock is unusual. It's alphabetical, his three initials AJN plus a Z." The manager swiftly found the locker with the odd lock, opened it, and returned to the desk, leaving Alan changing clothes in the locker room.

But this was all too much, and I was feeling beaten down by this superhuman effort to preserve his athletic identity. "I need to cancel our membership," I said with blunt resolve. The manager didn't try to dissuade me. It took him only a few keystrokes on his computer, and we would no longer be auto-billed monthly. We were no longer members. Done.

Within two weeks, we both began to feel the loss. I missed settling down on my mat behind the glass walls of the Pilates class with my lively teacher and her music, along with the regular classmates who had, over time, seemed like friends. I'd come to count on the rhythm of our fitness club days, and in some kind of magical thinking I'd imagined we could continue this way indefinitely. Now that my plateau had crumbled, I cherished it in retrospect.

And Alan missed the outlet of swimming, both physically and psychologically. Not having an athletic form of expression for the first time since high school, he felt the loss that went straight to the heart of his identity and purpose. I'd thought that at least he had the garden and the garage and the caterpillars, the chrysalides, and the butterflies, but our diminished weekly cycle without the health club proved that these and the monarch project, for him, were far from sufficient. He was despondent. He began shuffling around the house.

Another week passed. I decided to try a loving lie. "Here is a new idea," I told him. "If we were to rejoin the club, you could just hang your gym bag on the hook by the pool. No lock needed."

"Great idea!" he said.

I was amazed. This was the very thing he had stubbornly refused to do three times. But there is little to no logic in dementia, much less a sense of sequence, so we rejoined the fitness club. The first day, we celebrated afterward at Albertsons, toasting each other with our Starbucks lattes. To me, the stop-start experience underlined how loss is a shape shifter when your mate has dementia.

But there can be gains, too. I think of my last visit to my gynecologist, when she said to me, "You're so fit. How did you get these tight abs?" and I said, "I've been taking Pilates." I doubt if I'd taken it up, except I had to keep busy at the club at the exact same hour when Alan swam his laps. Sometimes caregiving brings an unexpected benefit.

Mainly, though, I think Alan's acceptance of change would not have taken place unless I pushed his old habit ("it's called a locker room") off its track. Sometimes you have to lose to gain, and this was one of those times. Shaken loose, we crafted a different version of our routine, thanks to a variant on the caregiver's technique of distracting a dementia patient, in this case by an application of withholding.

Every time we went to the club on this second round, I felt a renewed sense of gratitude for what we still had. Of course, this plateau, this sense of stability, wouldn't last forever. I had only negotiated a reprieve in a world where routine becomes erased by a progressive disease.

Traveling

PROGRESSIVE. MOVING FORWARD, into the future. Yet progress is such a loaded word.

On a Saturday in mid-April of 2019, an odd phenomenon of the moving-forward kind occurred in our garden: ten plump yellow-and-black caterpillars began a kind of walking migration, rippling along on their tiny feet. The caravan followed a westerly path along the red-brick border of the raised milkweed bed, heading toward our front porch.

This had happened once before, but not in such numbers. Now that I think about it, that last time was when Alan's condition first became apparent, two years ago, in early 2017. We were amazed, back then, when five caterpillars had traveled a distance of maybe 30 feet from the milkweed garden. We figured they were seeking protection from the elements under an overhanging roof.

This weekend would conclude with the unusual sight of ten caterpillars on the column of the front porch, forming their chrysalides side by side.

Two weeks later, on Sunday, May 5, and coinciding with Cinco de Mayo, we were having brunch and not on caterpillar-watch duty because not much happens in monarch world when it remains chilly outside. They stay still, sleeping in, until the sun warms the leaves under which they are dozing.

For most of our marriage, our Sunday routine had been to enjoy a leisurely home brunch and watch critters of all kinds. I set up breakfast at a table for two by the big front window—poached eggs on toast, more toast for jam, individual small pots of tea, fresh fruit in season. It might be oranges from our back yard, or figs from the north yard, or our pomegranates in the fall, their ruby pips in a compote with grapefruit sections and a sprinkling of sugar.

The front window has a wooden window seat, perfect for arraying the thick Sunday newspapers as we sort through them and pull out sections. Through the glass, we can watch squirrels cavorting around the big ash tree in the front yard. We also watch people strolling by with their dogs. This neighborhood, with its tree-lined streets and many historic homes, has been named as Orange County's best neighborhood for walking.

Inside our house, the Sunday newspapers reflect who we are, or in Alan's case, who he once was. I always go straight for the Book Reviews then scan the rest of the *New York Times* and the *Los Angeles Times*. In the past, Alan always headed straight for the opinion pages, paying special attention to national politics, a decades-long interest.

Sadly, though, these days he asks me with increasing frequency, "Who is this person?" He'll read a name aloud, and it might be a well-known member of Congress or a household name on every nightly newscast he watches routinely. He is losing the match-up of notable names with their roles in the national political scene, becoming disconnected from recognition of famous faces. The phrase "well known" no longer applies.

The same might be said of the Travel section.

It wasn't always this way. Once upon a time, we both read the Travel section first, passing it between us. We used to read about destinations with interest and intent because our next great adventure might be described in detail on the turn of a page. Also because during the first decade of our marriage, I'd published free-lance travel articles, and some included his photographs.

We'd traveled for adventure, and bylines, back then, as well as to delve into culture and history. We went diving in French Polynesia, Belize, Cozumel, Hawaii, and the Galapagos, and zip-lined in Mexico and Central America. We retraced his ancestral roots on a trip through Austria and Hungary. We reprised my 1965 college trip via rail pass through Spain. We made his science-guy's pilgrimage to the Greenwich Observatory and the equator monument, Mitad del Mundo, in Ecuador, as well as making a transit through the Panama Canal.

Alan was at home in or on the water in many modes, including an extended family vacation with his daughter and her in-laws on a multi-thousand-passenger cruise to Alaska. Our own preference was the 200-passenger-size craft necessary for river cruises, and since rivers were his specialty as a hydrologist, it's no surprise that he methodically checked off his bucket list of rivers: the Danube, the Elbe, the Rhine. We took a short cruise on the Seine between Normandy and Paris for my sixtieth birthday. Add the Yangtze, because our last big adventure by air, land, and waterways before dementia grounded us was three weeks in China.

Now, grounded we were, with international travel out of the question. But in December of 2018, I read about a new option in the travel section. It occurred to me that a domestic cruise might be safe for Alan, thereby avoiding the risk of him wandering away on foreign shore visits. He agreed with enthusiasm—we'd be travelling and back on the water!—so I reserved a cabin on an April 2019 cruise between Los Angeles and San Francisco, with stops in familiar places like Catalina and Santa Barbara. This was a cruise billed as Coastal California.

As the spring departure date neared, however, he continued to slide, and I began to fear he might become lost even in the relative safety of a cruise ship. Lost among a dozen floors and amid thousands of people. I considered how much more confused he was becoming and how his confusion was often expressed as rebellion. Even if he agreed not to leave the cabin without me, I could picture him wandering away, intentionally or not, if I so much as stepped into the shower. The upcoming cruise began to loom like a not-so-fun Easter egg hunt with me repeatedly searching for a misplaced husband.

I anguished over the decision, but then an emergency room visit cinched it. Alan fell, and I requested a doctor's note about his balance-caused injury. This justified trip-cancellation insurance. Otherwise, knowing expenses are relative when you are on the long journey with a loved one with dementia, I was ready to forfeit the cruise deposit anyway. Even as I was glad to get a refund, I knew it was small change compared to unknown healthcare costs on the horizon.

Finally, our exploring days were over. The travel sections, arrayed with other parts of the newspaper in the window seat during our Sunday brunches, were just a reminder of who we once were.

We had finished our Sunday breakfast, on that Cinco de Mayo of 2019, when the sun broke through the morning clouds.

We walked out the side door, where the steps mark the middle of the milkweed garden. Lo and behold, there was another caterpillar caravan underway, though only three of them this time, but Alan noticed that a fourth had veered south and was half way across the driveway in an unsafe move.

He picked it up and set it on the brick border wall, where it seemed to follow the trail of his kindred who had traveled this way before. We agreed that any day with a monarch rescue counts as a very good day.

Even as our life as a couple slips away, vestiges remain. One of these has taken on more importance, and, curiously, this is Alan's collection of ties. These days he has fewer reasons to wear a tie. Around the house he'll wear a T-shirt, but if we go out, he insists on a long-sleeved shirt with sleeves rolled up at the elbow and finished with a tie.

He'll wear one for any outing, say, dozing through a film or sitting in a physician's waiting room or dining at a cafe. From somewhere in his long-term, or maybe call it muscle memory, he is still capable of manipulating the long piece of fabric. Tying a tie is something he learned as a boy.

His collection began after a job promotion in his civil engineering days, when he took up the wearing of management-guy ties. Being a kind of gadfly in his office back then, he went for the playful twist of unexpected patterns, like the irreverence of Dilbert when that strip came along. Like most collections, his expanded through gifts and catalog orders and travel souvenirs.

These days when he chooses a tie and holds it in his hand, I think it helps him make a connection. He might ask, Who gave me this? Where did we buy it? Where are we going today? He picks a tie to... well, to tie in with an occasion. You could call it a ritual, his riffling through the tie rack in this process of selection.

Since I've known him, and to name only a half-dozen examples of this accessory ritual, Alan would wear a tie with a pattern of sea life to a members' night at the Aquarium of the Pacific, he'd choose one with profiles of airplanes on a day we were heading to LAX, and he'd don one with math or science symbols for classes when he was still teaching at the university.

Some of his ties feature antique maps, like the one we bought at the Royal Observatory in Greenwich, where he stood astride the historic Meridian Line. Some show patterns of tiny book covers, and he'd wear one of those to meetings of our co-ed neighborhood book club. He has two with Frank Lloyd Wright designs and wears them on trips to Chicago to see his daughter, who lives near the museum and former home of the famous architect.

These days, although my husband and I are often at odds over his getting dressed at all—and it can take five times as long as before, not counting shoes—the tie collection anchors him in a world he can no longer navigate. Somehow he still he manages to go through the looping and crossing over to create a perfect knot at his collar. It's a memoir waiting on a tie rack, a way of doubling back to the person he once was.

Happy Bummer of a Birthday

FROM NOW ON, I plan to celebrate my birthday as if it spans several days. My reasoning goes like this: The exact date is likely to veer off the rails, as it did on July 29, 2019, when it coincided with a Monday at the health club.

Leaving the house for any occasion involves many "No, wait!" moments as Alan forgets then suddenly remembers and looks for misplaced items, mostly things he doesn't need to bring along. He doesn't need a certain hat. He doesn't need his keys because I have mine, and his are lost somewhere in the house, anyway. We don't need to take his wallet because, chances are, it would be misplaced in the locker room.

On this particular day I had already packed a clean white towel in his sport bag. Then I noticed that he had draped a large peach guest towel over his arm. "Everyone brings white towels," he said. "I'll know this is mine."

"Okay…good idea." What the hell? I'm thinking. Why am I saving a good towel? For company that no longer comes for dinner, or the book group that no longer meets at our house?

After a final debate about what's needed today and what's not, we finally get rolling. Tense after today's extra-long negotiation, I focus on the road.

We are half-way to the gym when I glance his way and realize that he had changed out of the agreed-upon clothes and back into his filthy gardening shorts.

That's when I lose it and yell at the top of my lungs, "Happy birthday to me!" My outburst makes me feel better for a minute, but soon it's hangover-style worse, because when you lose it, the guilt zeros out the catharsis.

On the gym schedule, my Pilates class starts at 9:45. I am aware that deadlines are a bad idea when your mate has dementia. Arriving late, I grab the one remaining spot on the floor. I'm emotionally exhausted even before my workout begins.

The good towel does not make it home, of course, which I discover when I empty Alan's sport bag. Oh, well, no use fretting over the loss of a towel, it's just part of the cost of doing business, the business side of being a caregiver. Naturally, Alan doesn't remember that today is my birthday, but after that blowup and sad realization earlier this morning, I waste no energy fretting about that, either.

Home from the gym, I self-celebrate with a short nap and a long read. Mid-afternoon, I decide to run a few errands with Alan along. A joint excursion works okay if the expedition is kept loose and is not under time pressure.

So errand-running we go, to the local (thankfully small) hardware store, then a stop for coffee at Starbucks, and on to the last stop, Trader Joe's. There I spot two gifts to buy for myself: a bouquet of multicolored flowers and a purple, pansy faced Miltonia orchid. Thanks to the flowers, with maybe a boost from the caffeine, my birthday starts feeling like a celebration!

Then a decision is needed about dinner. This is the first year when we have not made special plans for my birthday, but dining out apart from the most casual cafe has become too difficult. For this birthday dinner, I decide on a whole chicken take-out with the next-day benefit of leftovers. Our last stop about 5 p.m. is at Polly's Pies, where we order the roast chicken with sides and two slices of pie.

We await the take-out order sitting side by side on an oak settee in the lobby. After a couple of minutes, Alan leans over and laces his fingers through mine, then slides closer so we are thigh to thigh. I feel his warmth, and rest my head against his shoulder. And it all comes back … a rush of love and belonging together, the wellspring of our quarter century together, almost a third of my life, on a birthday turning out not so bad after all.

That moment on my birthday, when we sat side by side on the restaurant's oak settee, was a gift of grace in an increasing swirl of chaos. I'd caught a glimpse of Alan's sweetness, a dear trait of the man I love, a side almost eclipsed by his illness. But not quite.

If someone devised a Tenderness Quotient Scale, my husband would rank high on that scale. Despite his bluster, he is one of those sensitive people—perhaps overly sensitive to cold, heat, and sudden sounds. Strange cats and dogs are drawn to him, and hearing about anyone in desperate straits not only makes him sad but, whenever possible, eager to help them.

We had been dating for a couple of weeks when my mother noticed this quality in him. It happened on the day I introduced them to each other. We were standing on her big front porch, and when she came to the door, I said, "Mom, I'd like you to meet Alan."

It was as though the two of them bonded right there on the porch, maybe recognizing this sensitive quality in each other. Later that day she told me her initial impression. "There is something about him," she said, "a kindness."

My very sensitive mother, who I'd say had a tenderness antenna, soon came to love my husband as a son.

I was reminded of this special quality today, but also of how easy it is for us to lose sight of someone's best side when we're fighting the terrible disease-symptoms that are taking over their mind.

He surprised me this morning by plucking a tiny camellia from a bush on the shady north side of the house, where milkweeds do not grow. He brought the flower into my office and quietly set it on my desk, just inches away from where I was working at my Mac. I looked up at him, over at the camellia, and it felt like a chime rang through me ... because of this gift of a tiny pink bud.

Setting aside for a moment all the difficulties we face now, like how they give rise to frustration and anger, and his need to assert his independence set against my need to survive the long night of this disease, one thing that brings us back to our shared center is our appreciation of nature, especially nature in miniature.

The caterpillars evoke our protective response. It must sound strange to say I experience sentiments toward an insect, but tenderness is a gift wherever you find it, whether in the face of an infant or the round eyes of a kitten ... or in a newbie caterpillar the length of my fingernail.

When I sometimes say aloud in a moment of enthusiasm, "I just love these little guys," Alan has countered with, "Well, I can't say I love them, exactly, but I do care for them." It's an assertion of his science-guy's precision. When he speaks this way, offsetting my emotional outpourings, I am glad to still get a glimpse of this discerning and highly intelligent man.

I am grateful for such unexpected moments and the surprise I feel when they arise. For a while, I know there will be more.

Today, though, I am grateful for his gift of the small pink camellia, now floating in a silver pill cup.

Chapter 5
MY BELOVED WRECKING BALL

Busy Hands

DECLINE IN JUDGMENT is another behavior caused by the deterioration of a brain with dementia. In our home, it looks like we are stuck in the middle of this phase.

The more kinds of mechanisms and devices you have around the house, the greater the chance that your husband with dementia will disable them. It's as if he's reverted to, say, a high school shop class. Your loved one doesn't mean to wreck things, of course, but when you consider the lure of "something to do," it makes sense. A basic human need.

After his driver's license became invalid, Alan began casting around for opportunities to take action, to keep busy. Gardening didn't fill his days. Because he's not the kind of person to sit around for hours and read or watch TV (especially with his ability to follow a plot so diminished), he began looking for objects to handle and touch and repair ... even if that something didn't need repairing.

As an engineer by training, he seeks objects to take apart, rebuild, and improve. Optimize. He has now begun to wreck things in myriad ways. Chances are that after the first time, this behavior will happen again. This is because repetition becomes ingrained in a person with dementia.

During the years of our marriage, I have always deferred to him as the mechanically-and-electronically-inclined man of the house. The exception is my personal computer, which I am, it's fair to say, quite capable of managing myself.

One problem now is that because Alan doesn't remember recent advances in technology, he regresses to what he knew years ago. Take the TV. One day when I was not in the room, he forgot how to use the remote. Rather than call me to remind him ("I am here to remind you ..." being one of my handy refrains), he simply started pulling out cables from the back of the set, sticking them back in every which way. Goodbye, satellite service.

I phoned the tech helpline and tried my best to follow the instructions dictated by the telephone advice rep, and when that didn't solve the problem, I was offered a house call. Trouble was, the first availability was five days later. That meant almost a week without one of the activities that adds stability and structure to our evenings. Alan dotes on the evening news and political commentary. Even if the content barely registers, watching TV news remains his nightly ritual. It was a crabby week around the house until satellite service was finally restored.

A similar thing happened with our home WiFi.

In his current state, Alan forgets that we have a router, and have had it for some years, so old terms like "dial-up" come to mind and mire him in the past. When he forgot how to both log onto his laptop and key in his password, despite its being written on a Post-It he could easily see, he turned to an outmoded mechanical solution to the problem.

There sat the router, an alluring mechanical presence with its tempting cables sticking out. As I see it, the boy living inside Alan set about taking it apart, maybe to see how it worked. Gone was our home WiFi, and, most inconveniently, on a weekend, which meant our provider could only fit in a house call three days later.

The next casualty was the automatic lawn sprinkler.

The system we use is as environmentally sensitive as you can get and still have a lawn, meaning, a sensor keeps the water use at a minimum. The control is housed in a gray plastic box the size of a small briefcase. It's attached to one wall of the garage, and when you open the lid, you see all the dials and gadgets that control the settings—days of the week, location, and duration. Ahh, so many tempting widgets to mess with, and mess with them he did. Until I noticed that the front lawn and back lawn were dying.

The milkweed for the monarchs didn't show any distress, being a weed, but the rest of the yard was obviously suffering. It had to be caused by the watering system not acting automatically anymore, so I called Mel, the specialist, and a few hours later he had reset and reactivated all the stations around the house. Then I duct-taped the irrigation box closed and also affixed a hand-lettered warning, Please Do Not Touch! I was hoping such words in bold print might give him pause.

And yet I knew. I knew I had to accept his destructive behavior as one of his "new jobs." Just so they understood, I warned service people like Mel that I'd likely be calling them again. Sure, I'd be paying for multiple house calls, but such expenses would be a bargain if it meant Alan could remain engaged a little longer in our so-called normal world.

The automatic garage door mechanism was the next victim of my beloved human wrecking ball. It seems that one day he glanced up at the ceiling and decided to modify the light in the automatic opener. He wanted to make it brighter. This might have been a response to another aspect of his dementia, deterioration in his visual cortex, which makes objects harder to recognize, perhaps at times harder to see. In pursuit of better light, he disabled part of the mechanism to optimize it, and in a typical moment of distraction, walked away and forgot about finishing the task.

I had no clue, of course, so when the garage door didn't shut I was puzzled about what might be the cause. I made a call to Chris, our garage door guy, who squeezed us into his schedule the next day. When he saw how my husband had rearranged the mechanism, and knowing about Alan's condition, he quietly showed me what had happened and how to fix it should it happen again. Chris said he understood such a misguided effort. His own mother has dementia.

A month later, Alan came up with a variant on his first garage door project. *Aha*, I thought, I know what to do, but this time it was different. Now the garage wouldn't open. Fortunately, our car was parked under the carport. Then I had an epiphany, of sorts. I began to see past the hassle of scheduling another repair.

This was a gift in disguise. It gave me an excuse to back out of the neighborhood's quarterly garage sale planned for the coming weekend. Our folding tables for display were in the garage. Alan usually looked forward to the garage sales, always getting into the spirit of people stopping by and chatting. Ordinarily, it amounted to two fun and lively mornings, us sitting on our folding chairs with me handling the business side. By now, however, he was becoming so reactive toward things that I knew he would be holding objects back with a remark like, "I'll keep this, after all." The social side of the garage sale would be a problem, too. His conversations were likely to careen wildly off topic.

The delay over the stuck garage door gave me another carrot to dangle. The city's next legal garage sale would be three months away. "We'll have more old things to sell then," I lied, giving him something to look forward to.

One way to pause a destruction derby is by bringing in an expert. When Alan suddenly, and with no excuse, started peeling bark off the giant ash tree in our front yard, ripping away huge slabs and obviously harming the tree, I asked him to stop. He ignored me. I called the gardener and requested an emergency house call. My husband was in the act when the gardener arrived. "No, no, no," he said. "What you're doing will badly hurt it. You might kill the tree!" To which I said, "Let's get that in writing so I can show it to him when he forgets." And that's what the gardener did, scribbling, DO DO NOT PEEL BARK on a creased old invoice that stood in for a sort of prescription pad.

I'll mention one more example that shows how no object is safe. One day I noticed that he had attached a padlock to the belt loop of his favorite tan walking shorts. By closing the lock, which he'd found open in the garage (the lock's short hasp open but no key in sight), he sealed the fate of those shorts. The lock means the shorts can no longer be laundered. How about removal with a bolt cutter, you might ask. Well, the hasp is so short that hacking through it would destroy the shorts. Cut away the belt loop? No belt, no iPhone holster, and his iPhone held my secret tracking device. Oh, well. No more walking shorts, not this pair anyway.

These are a few variants on destructive behavior, and each time I've had to resist giving an eye-roll and blurting out, "Are you kidding me?"

But in the end—because this is one of my discoveries about living through the process of being a caregiver-spouse—there are gifts hidden in some of the most frustrating moments. There was the gift of the delayed garage sale, of course, but a better example was the happy departure of Alan's laptop. It had been a source of trouble for some months, ranging from the costly Trike he'd ordered online to inappropriate messages he sometimes posted on Facebook…when he remembered how to use it.

Then a new series of problems revealed gift-bestowing potential: He forgot how to turn on the laptop, couldn't find the little power button on his Mac. Forgot how to open the browser or handle email or access his files. These were the frustrations that had led him, twice, to disable the router.

So the next time he became frustrated and walked away from the laptop. I seized the moment. "Your laptop needs repair," I said as I unplugged it, packed it up, and said I would take it to the Apple dealer. Actually, I hid it away.

Later, when he would occasionally ask where it was, I'd say, "Oh, we sent it off to the Mac repair shop. I'll check and see if it's ready." Of course, it wasn't at the shop but stored in the back of my closet. Soon he became accustomed to not using a computer. In time, he forgot to ask.

Eat Early and Often

WE TEND to take food for granted as part of the ebb and flow of a marriage. That is, until one spouse is placed on a restricted diet, say, or a change like dementia alters the rhythm of sharing meals. Alan's behavioral changes ended many years of pleasurable dining out. The end of that long run has now arrived. Except for an occasional drive-thru, we always eat at home.

The psychology of food is complicated and rooted in our childhood. My husband grew up with a single working mom who always tried to make ends meet. I was raised with never a worry about an empty refrigerator, and because our house was next door to my grandparents' house, family gatherings involving meals were frequent and bountiful.

But I do remember when I was in elementary school and my parents' marriage was disintegrating. That's when I began to pay keen attention to the menus of school lunches. Each week's cafeteria menu was published in the *Long Beach Press Telegram* on Mondays, and I'd root through pages crammed with local news and advertisements until I found it. Then my mom and I would read it together. My favorite cafeteria dish was Sloppy Joes.

Looking back, I think that knowing the details of each day's lunch menu helped me through a time of uncertainty, one culminating in my parents' divorce in the late 1950s at a time when divorce was far from common. The school menu was a source of comfort and predictability, the daily lunch, a kind of reassurance that our family would continue, a stepping-stone from one day to the next. It seems not unlike my life today, except these days, dinner is that stepping stone.

Although often I have lapsed into the role of chicken take-out queen, I've long been a fair cook with a smallish repertoire of dishes. In recent months, as if I'm channeling the idea of the school cafeteria menu, I've been planning the week's dinner menus like my life depends on it. I shop for ingredients with serious intent. Lists are so satisfying when things are falling apart.

In recent months, I've been delving into complicated recipes and losing myself trying out various cuisines and techniques, from French to Italian, from crepes to Chicken Vesuvio. Who knew I'd take up such elaborate projects comparatively late in life? And it's not just a creative escape; it's interactive. I can count on Alan's response. He's never been a picky eater, anyway, but now he enjoys my new concoctions and showers me with praise.

Recipes are one of my anchors in the tidal surge of our days. In the morning when I awaken disoriented, I might ask myself: What's for dinner tonight? If I'm short on ingredients, there are always eggs, so maybe I'll make a stand-by frittata with whatever accents of produce I happen to have around. Produce has other applications, too. It may sound weird, but as an extension of this culinary dabbling I've turned to making lists at night to quiet my mind. That is, not by counting sheep but by picturing and enumerating varieties of fruits or vegetables in rhythmic alpha lists (A is for Apricot, B is for banana ... all the way to W is for watermelon, allowing myself to skip X, Y, and Z). It works almost every time, and soon I drop off into the reward of a few hours of oblivion.

Partly in my mind (like recipes) and partly through the cycle of creating daily meals, a focus on food gives me the illusion these days that I have some control over our out-of-control life. Both productive and practical, planning and cooking dinner is not unlike the pleasure of watching our caterpillars munching on milkweed, which diverts us from the fact of Alan's decline. We are all chomping away, and it's on to another new day.

It was the spring of 2019, and on the refrigerator, secured by a magnet, was a flyer announcing a neighborhood Town Hall meeting. It would take place a short walk away. Alan, who had long been outspoken about local politics, wanted to attend and speak out, to express himself as he has done with confidence for decades.

How dismal it felt when I had to redirect my husband away from a favorite activity of his, one in which he had always taken pride. I had to make a case that he should avoid public speaking.

That same morning he'd said, "I had a strange dream last night," and in the retelling, he became upset because his dreams are more vivid lately and some are hitting him hard. He went on to describe how, like a stand-up comic, he'd dreamed he was telling jokes and his audience was cracking up with laughter.

Piggy-backing on this, I offered an interpretation of how his dream might connect with the upcoming Town Hall event. "Maybe the dream was prompted by the flyer for the meeting," I said, "but maybe laughter isn't what you want from your audience."

I had already, and as diplomatically as possible, suggested that he not attend the meeting. I knew if he did go, then he would be compelled by long habit to hold forth at length and firmly express his views. He'd try to win any argument.

In the old days, he could do this like a wizard and always count on a respectful response from an audience. In his dual career as civil engineer and college math instructor, he'd served as an expert witness, given countless lectures at the university, and spoken before large gatherings, such as the American Society of Civil Engineers.

When it came to public speaking, Alan is someone who rarely needs notes. He's a master of improv. When we were first dating, we attended one of his formal professional events together, and he was asked on the spot to stand in for a speaker who had cancelled at the last minute. I was blown away by how articulate and relaxed Alan was pulling off this impromptu high-wire act.

But in recent months, and increasingly so, he has been resorting to all-purpose phrases, fillers, non sequiturs that don't fit the conversation. In response to a comment someone might make on just about any point he might reply, "Just imagine that," or, "I am just trying to brighten your day."

Now here comes the Town Hall meeting, which he wants to attend and participate in. But I don't want him to get confused and falter. I picture him stepping up to a microphone as he has done

countless times , but now his words and phrases will be fragmented, off-topic, and he will ramble ... until someone in the audience
who is unaware of his condition is likely to interrupt, maybe rude-
ly, and insist that he sit down. I want to spare him this because
even if I come along, I cannot help him.

Facing this prospect, I say, "Maybe it's not such a good idea
for you to speak at the meeting. I'm guessing that the information
you once had at your fingertips is ... well, rusty."

I am thinking, Please don't go. It will turn out badly, but instead I pose a question: "You wouldn't want to be embarrassed,
would you?"

To which he replies, "I don't care if I embarrass myself. I
won't even know if I do."

Thankfully, in the end, he decides not to go.

Touched

TOUCH IS A TRICKY PART of a journey through the land of dementia because we all seek contact as a way of conveying our love
to someone. Alan and I have always held hands, and I relish this
expression of affection.

Then a few months ago, as we sat together one evening while
watching our TV programs, Alan began tucking his palm under
the edge of my thigh. I thought it was sweet and reassuring to both
of us, being connected like that. He began carrying the gesture
over to when we were driving or sleeping, and I liked falling asleep
with the flat, warm edge of his hand barely wedged under me.

Around the same time, he also began giving me gentle little
pats when he walked past me. "Thank you," I began saying, showing my appreciation for these signals of love. Soon it settled into a
habit of his touch and my response, to me a welcome layer added
to our days together.

In one of my email updates, I reported this development
to his daughter. "I see another upside of your dad's condition," I
wrote, "He is becoming tenderly affectionate."

That was a couple of months ago, and for the past couple of
weeks he has begun stroking me in a way that seems compulsive.
Rubbing. As before, it happens while we're watching television, or
we're driving, or we're in bed when we are dropping off to sleep.
If he is restless and rubbing me, and I am trying to fall asleep, it
blocks me from that last delicious slide into unconsciousness.

I've tried saying, "Honey, that tickles," which stops him. Until he starts up again. I've also tried, "Alan, would you please stop that?" He gets it briefly, but soon he forgets and begins again. I now know how a cat feels when its coat is rubbed the wrong way. It can make you crazy. I'll have to consult my Alzheimer's coach or look for a workaround in my snooze-alarm dreams.

And every workaround or problem deferred gives me hope I'll find a way forward, whether it concern's Alan's dementia or our caterpillars or my effort to survive.

Take today, for example. For the past three weeks, we have hosted a monarch caterpillar in our living room. You might wonder why a chrysalis is suspended in a mesh cage inside a window, rather than progressing through its metamorphosis outdoors.

Southern California rarely gets rain, but in this month of February 2019 it has rained day after day, from sprinkles to pounding downpours sometimes accompanied by slashing winds. A few monarchs sometimes show up early and lay eggs in February, which happened this year. A couple of the eggs hatched, and the caterpillars ate their way through four molting stages (or instars), then a couple made it to the penultimate stage, a celadon green chrysalis dangling by its cremaster, a tiny black thread.

For this phase, most of the caterpillars chose safe locations, in some cases on the wooden trellises we provide, but one made an odd choice we had never seen before. It formed its green chrysalis on a milkweed leaf. This was risky for two reasons: first, because another caterpillar might eat that same leaf, or, second, the leaf might become dry and fall off before the chrysalis has time to develop. Either way, it would cause a fatal plunge to the ground where likely a predator like a cockroach would dispatch the chrysalis and the creature inside it.

After so many years of minding monarchs, we naturally had a contingency plan. I retrieved the rescue cage from the attic, then carefully cut through the black thread supporting the chrysalis and reattached it under the net lid of the cage with a little alligator clip. The net cage with its temporary resident fit perfectly atop a low bookshelf by a window.

Every day we checked the progress of our houseguest, and on March 16, a female butterfly emerged. Later that morning we carried the cage outside to the front patio. I unzipped the top, folded it back, and the butterfly's instinct urged her to climb higher and higher with her tiny claspers. She reached the top of the open cage and had what she needed, an elevated launch pad. Once in position and with a vigorous flapping of wings, she soared away into a clear spring sky.

The monarch's chrysalis phase lasts about two weeks. Sometimes during the past week or so, after checking on the progress of this developing butterfly, I'd wait for a few minutes and think about the chrysalis inside its protective cage. Although deprived of open air for the duration, it had other advantages, like safety from predators and south-facing sunlight. While I was standing in front of the bookcase, a phrase came to mind: "A Clean, Well-Lighted Place," the title of a short story by Ernest Hemingway.

It occurred to me then that Alan and I are living in a kind of protective net cage. For now, I think, this is not a bad variation on what would otherwise be our normal life. We are safe, cocooned even, inside a cozy home bordered by a special garden. And if the day comes when I can no longer care for him here—if he becomes a resident in the best memory care facility we can find—then I hope and pray he will be comfortable, safe, well-cared for and protected, in a clean, well-lighted place, a home away from home.

Touch, or not touching, comes into play again. It is May 24, 2019, and I am grateful for a blue-sky day, glad because yesterday was both overcast and one of the low points between us.

Looking back, I feel ashamed. There were voices raised, out-of-room stomping, doors slamming. He had baited me, repeatedly, and I overreacted. He broke a favorite glass object of my mother's that I'd asked him not to touch. He refused to shower, again, and I called him dirty. I am the one who knows better. I have absorbed the rules for a caregiver of a loved one with dementia and it is my responsibility to follow them. *Redirect, distract, summon patience, walk away.* Moreover, it was up to me to apologize.

At the end of that bad day, at dinner last night, I raised a toast with a glass of cider, now our preferred and minimally five-percent alcoholic beverage. I said, "To a better day tomorrow."

In bed, as we were both reading before going to sleep, I saw tears on Alan's face. I reached over and patted his arm, trying to offer some kind of loving reassurance.

"I thought you'd written me off," he said.

"Oh, no, never ...." I felt my heart would break.

In the morning when it seemed that calm had returned, when we had settled back into our more-or-less normal state, the conflict of the previous day was still whirling through my mind, so I said, "I'd like to talk with you about acceptance."

"Acceptance?" he shot back. "What does that even mean?"

He was standing in the doorway of my small home office as I tried to explain my intention. "Our lives have changed," I began, "and we need to accept these new circumstances. New limitations. I'm afraid there is no going back to the way we once were. So please help me accept these changes. Please help me help you."

"I'll try."

Later that day, another chrysalis we have been monitoring, this one positioned under a window ledge, emerges. At first glance, she looks normal ... it's that first impression, not unlike when someone has a brief conversation with Alan and initially he seems fine.

But after this butterfly begins drying her wings, it becomes clear to me that her wings are damaged. One is twisted, and when she tries to fly she lands crumpled in the driveway.

I run to her and reach down, and she climbs on my finger. Now I am sitting with her in the sunlight, turning my hand to direct the warmth on her. She unfurls her orange, black, and white wings as best she can, and just then Alan walks by and she takes off in front of him. He cries out joyfully, "Whoa! What's that?"

"Our rescue butterfly," I say. "She tried to fly, but can't." Now she lands, sprawled on the concrete. I pick her up again.

When this happens to a damaged butterfly, we try to give it as comfortable a brief life as possible before we quickly and, you might say humanely, bring it to an end. So now here I am, sitting on the back porch with a wounded monarch on my finger. Soon I will place her on a nearby nectar plant so, for a while, she can sip and bide her time.

These moments of what might be called an interspecies connection are some of the most serene times in my current life. I feel as if time is standing still. The butterfly is nearly weightless, yet I am aware of her weight as she opens and closes her wings, of the sensation of her tiny claspers holding onto me for support. Her touch evokes in me a deep feeling of affection.

Maybe it's because I feel emotionally bruised now, vulnerable and torn after yesterday's medley of conflicts with Alan—my anger over him breaking a precious object, and when he repeatedly baited me as if to watch me sputter and react—but this female butterfly seems like an intermediary sent to help me recover my love for my husband.

These days my true feelings for him are too often buried under worry and impatience and, to my shame, blocked by anger.

Today I am grateful for the damaged butterfly tapping into my closed-off wellspring of empathy.

The Greatest Workaround of All

BACK IN 2017, our first approach to Alan's memory loss had been to consider whether depression was the cause. To determine this, he began seeing a psychiatrist. He was still her patient two years later when one particular session led to my most radical attempt so far at diverting him in our journey with dementia.

By this time, I was regularly sitting in for half of his session, in part as a reality check. The doctor had just asked him the obligatory question: "Have you had thoughts about hurting yourself."

For the first time, my husband answered, "Yes."

Startled, I must have sat up straight. The psychiatrist didn't show surprise and I'm sure therapists are trained not to. I flashed on ways Alan might try to hurt himself. I had already managed to remove the guns from the house, but this wasn't about guns. I was about to hear that he had a different plan entirely. I listened with alarm as he proceeded to tell us the exact way he intended to take his own life.

We have beautiful trees on our property, and the one in front is the aforementioned ash tree, eighteen feet in circumference, as tall as a four-story building.

Nestled among three massive branches is a tree house he had built by a carpenter for visits by the grandchildren, now grown. A wooden ladder leads to a hatch, which we always keep locked, but once the hatch is unlocked, both the tree house and the tree's high, upper branches are accessible.

That day in the session with the psychiatrist while I sat listening, stunned, Alan explained how he foresaw the scene of his own demise. He planned to jump from one of the high branches. Take a fatal dive onto the concrete driveway below.

"I keep picturing it," he said. "The idea of the beautiful tree gives me a peaceful feeling, knowing I can take my life that way when I want to."

I froze. How could he conflate the idea of peace and our beautiful tree with ending his life splayed on concrete? Years ago, we had discussed, in theory, the possibility of a physician-assisted demise if one of us was diagnosed as terminal. That diagnosis was here, but assisted departure did not apply to a patient with dementia who was not of sound mind. Alan didn't fully understand that he had dementia.

The psychiatrist drew him out further, while I silently screamed *no, no, no*, envisioning the trauma of what our neighbors' children might witness. Then my mind spun further to the possibility that if he took such a dive, he might instinctively try to right himself, like a cat, and survive but with massive injuries.

A frightening pathway had opened in that therapy session.

As soon as I got home, I phoned Audrey, my Alzheimer's coach, to tell her about Alan's plan. She tried to calm me down, saying that most Alzheimer's patients lack the focus and resolve to do such a deed, though, she added, "And yet some do." I knew such a drastic action as diving out of a tree would be almost impossible for me to prevent unless he never left my sight. Otherwise, what could I do? Install an alarm that would sound if he entered the front yard? He could disable such a device in about a minute.

I needed to redirect him, somehow steer him away from his fixation with the tree.

And then a postcard arrived in the mail.

Alan and I had never favored traditional cemetery arrangements. Far from it, and to me, Evelyn Waugh's satirical novel *The Loved One*, about Forest Lawn, always comes to mind. But Alan and I had talked about alternative possibilities. He had arranged to scatter his mother's ashes at sunset during a skydive jump. My father had asked me to scatter his ashes in a remote desert area he loved. As scuba divers, Alan and I had read with some interest about our ashes being used as part of an artificial reef, but we hadn't researched it any further.

And yet ... when the postcard from the memorial park arrived, I didn't throw it away. I gave it a serious second glance. It was an announcement for a new memory garden, recently dedicated at a cemetery near our home. As shown in the color photo on the postcard, on one side of the garden stood a mosaic wall, its visual theme a landscape with a river flowing past a curving, verdant bank. A river motif, I thought, as if it had Alan's name on it, as if it reflected his hydrology specialty as a civil engineer.

The mosaic wall overlooked a garden with pathways, and flowering plants and even a bubbling brook ... yes, an artificial brook, like a scene from *The Loved One*, but despite this cliché of a device, the park struck me as serenely lovely in its own way.

Now, I reflected, still holding the postcard, I had a mission, to distract my husband from his idea of effecting a final exit by jumping from out of the ash tree for a shock-factor trip to eternity.

I made an appointment to see the memorial garden on a day when Ryan was present at our house and it seemed even more appealing in person. Once I had returned home, I expressed interest, enthusiasm, even, and Alan agreed to come with me and take a look. As we stood facing the mosaic wall with its river scene, where I'd learned we could have a little niche for ashes for two, I said, "I want us to be here together, someday."

And I did a bit of marketing, too, about how we would be among the first so we could choose our own preferred section of the mosaic. I tried to set a scene, to superimpose a new image not of the ash tree but here. And I talked about how whether he or I should pass away first, the other one could come to this lovely garden and sit on a carved stone bench facing the mosaic of a flowing river. *River.* I must have said it a dozen times.

In short, Alan bought into the idea. And on our first visit to the cemetery that didn't feel like a cemetery to us, I took photographs, including one of him facing, as if contemplating, the wall.

And so we made the arrangements and bought our niche for two—something I had never, ever, imagined I would do. In the coming weeks and months, I would sometimes mention the memory garden and our special section of the river scene, and we'd even stop by sometimes, on the way to or from an errand. My all-time greatest workaround seemed to be, well, working out, because except for one close call a few months later, Alan stopped obsessing about the tree in our front yard.

Chapter 6
THE CRITTERS OF SUMMER

Lessons Learned, Lessons Shared

As EACH MONTH grinds by, I more fully understand the sustenance I gain from my support group. It's like breathing fresh air after being shut up in a stuffy room, like gulping a glass of water when you didn't realize you were thirsty. In today's meeting, I find out that I had a specific thirst and didn't know how to quench it.

This is another second Tuesday of the month, my caregiver-covered half-day when I try to pack in everything that needs doing. When I arrive at the support group slightly late and somewhat frazzled, I grab an empty chair, take out my pen and the small lime green notebook I'm using for my notes for this diary. What is my personal problem today? The issue of Alan's escalating anger.

Today we have a new member whom I'll call Sheryl. After the attendance sheet has made its way around the tables, Audrey, our group leader, asks Sheryl to introduce herself, explain which family member she is caring for, and describe her situation. When Sheryl comes to the third part, it's as if her words are springing directly from my head.

"He is angry at me all the time," she says, referring to her husband. "Day in and day out, I am assaulted by his rage. It is continually directed at me because I am there. I can't get away from it. I can hardly stand it."

We hear Audrey's advice as she makes eye contact around the room, because this issue is for everyone to hear. It's one of the key issues in our support group. "This woman needs to find help," Audrey says. "She needs respite." Audrey adds that she will contact Sheryl separately with a few suggestions for home caregiver services she might want to call.

When it is my turn, I begin by saying, "What Sheryl said exactly describes what I am facing right now. My husband starts firing snarky remarks at me as soon as he wakes up, and it builds all day. It's almost like, well, paranoia. He rages over swallowing his meds, taking a shower, leaving the house for an appointment. Anger is his job, and it's aimed full blast at me."

"So ..." Audrey begins slowly, "as I recall, you have one afternoon each week with caregiver coverage?" I say yes, to which she raises an eyebrow. "Then," she adds, "I'd say it's time to add at least a second day. Maybe two."

"I can see that," I reply, "the need for a second day, but ..."

"But what?"

"It must be a consistent day in order to book someone."

"Go on."

"And a day of the week I can justify so he won't fight me."

I am speaking my thoughts aloud, of course, working through a decision. This is the dynamic of such a group, a kind of therapy, and I feel it happening, the opening of the floodgates.

And it dawns on me: "He's always respected the excuse of 'business,'" I say, then I add, "I have a professional writers' group I've worked with for many years, but they only meet one Saturday a month." It was the group I'd had to abandon months ago.

"One Saturday, four Saturdays—he won't know the difference," Audrey says. "I'd arrange for regular coverage on all Saturdays and use the other three every month for time that you need, mainly getting away to regain your center and distance yourself from his anger."

I picture myself in a getaway moment with J.S. Bach on the car audio, and my heart lifts at the thought of restoring my equilibrium, regaining strength to gin up more patience. I have received a take-away today. Though it seems obvious now, I can't help but wonder why didn't I think of this before? Is it because I still feel it is my responsibility to be with my husband and not delegate even more of his care to a stranger? Or maybe because we caregiver spouses learn to adapt to circumstances, as if worsening conditions have a way of creeping up on you.

And as I tell this story now, writing it down two days after the support group session, it strikes me that this is what I'm hoping my book is about. Hearing about another person's experience has helped me. Maybe by reading my story it will help someone else, perhaps another caregiver spouse.

B is for Bug

Thump! I wake up in the middle of the night and see lights blazing throughout the house. I pad barefoot into the kitchen, where I find Alan in shorts and slippers, bending over something small, picking it up with a scrunched paper towel.

"What was that *sound*?"

"A bug," he says. "A big bug. I stomped on it. Here." He holds up the wadded paper. "Want a look?"

"No, thanks," I mumble, tamping down my resentment at again being awakened from an exhausted sleep. Sleep is getting hard to come by these days. The night before, he had leg cramps from ill-advised excessive swimming, and his cramps repeatedly woke us both. The night before that, he was on a night prowl and accidentally dropped a heavy book near my ear. Tonight, I've been ripped from sleep over the noisy execution of a cockroach.

Not all insects, in fact few, are lovable. I am no stranger to roaches. During the 1980s, I lived in the nation's largest city when the introduction of Combat bait stations in Manhattan came into the market as a kind of miracle. These vermin are rarely seen in our house, except this month when Edison has been working in our neighborhood. Maybe this critter, evicted by workmen, shimmied up a pipe and found its way into our kitchen. I know the roach has friends, because this isn't the first time lately that Alan has gone big bug hunting in the wee hours.

It's the nocturnal version of his main day job—his Bad-Bug-Crushing Crusade.

This takes place in the milkweed garden. To our disgust, we once saw a roach eating a monarch chrysalis like an apple, the damage done before we could drive it off. A more benign target for Alan's bad-bug vigilance is the aphids. When I can steer him into the garden, it gives me a break from the constant vigil and summoning of patience.

Aphids, being yellow and the size of pinheads, make them easy prey for a human hunter because they don't try to escape but simply hang there, quivering. They keep trying to colonize our milkweed, which obstructs the free movement of our caterpillars. It isn't that aphids directly harm our animals, but I wouldn't want to be a baby caterpillar facing a blob of that aphid-stuff as I was hungrily heading for a tender leaf. At the very least, those vermin are encroaching on prime monarch real estate. Plus, aphids are ugly and detract from the joy of caterpillar observation.

Alan also stalks the red and black milkweed bugs the size of a fat pencil tip that land in droves on our milkweed, where they mate and lay eggs. To evict them, he does a grab, drop, smash-on-the-concrete job. Between the aphids and the red-blacks, you could say that, bug-by-bug, he has a renewable source of activity, perpetually addressing the need for *something to do* for a man who scoffs at jigsaw puzzles and games.

Who knew that our milkweed garden would prove doubly therapeutic, not only attracting monarchs, but also providing infestations that engage my husband? In Bad Bug season, being nearly year-round, he heads to the garden first thing most mornings. After he sets up a little stool with a seat made of camouflage-pattern fabric, he begins aphid removal with an improvised tool: a piece of aluminum wide enough for him to grip, yet narrow enough for him to move in surgically close and strip away the tiny yellow bugs that form clusters on the milkweed stems.

This weird but meaningful work is his job, and I never interfere. Dispatching the bugs provides immediate, quantifiable results. I sometimes silently compare it to his former routine of grading student math papers, semester after semester. Purposeful, renewable work.

So when I think of the beautiful monarch and the annoying aphid and the pesky red-black bug, and of how good and bad bugs are all a part of our life, what comes to mind is a quote from Ralph Waldo Emerson. It goes like this:

> *Cultivate the habit of being grateful for every good thing that comes to you, and to give thanks continuously. And because all things have contributed to your advancement, you should include all things in your gratitude.*

What Kind of Predator is This?

According to the World Health Organization website, "The boundaries between different forms of dementia are indistinct and mixed forms often co-exist."

I HAVE LONG assumed that Alan's dementia has a name, and that name is Alzheimer's. Odds are for most dementia patients, that's the right name. An estimated eighty percent of dementia cases are Alzheimer's. I've been all in with using this term, partly because this is the name of the association that has had my back and sponsored the support group serving as my lifeline since 2017.

But this type of affliction has other names, too, even if its surname is Dementia. Sometimes it takes several years before enough symptoms develop to determine exactly what the alternate affliction is.

I remember the first time I attended an introductory seminar at a local chapter of the Alzheimer's Association, which offered three free classes designed to help family caregivers come to terms with behavioral changes in their loved ones.

We were shown a video at the introductory class, an animation portraying the progression of this "slow fatal disease of the brain ..." The animation, which is disarmingly effective with its continuous series of stick-figure cartoons, shows the relentless spread of plaques and tangles as they invade the different regions of the brain and compromise brain functions.

The narrator toured us through this terrible road map, whereby the abnormal proteins aggregate in the area called the hippocampus (seat of new or short-term memory). Next stop is where language is processed, then the damage moves on to the frontal area of the brain, the region of logic and solving problems. The next destination of this predatory disease is the area where emotions are regulated, causing loss of control over moods. Finally, the oldest memories are destroyed, and in the end-stage so are the regulation of breathing and function of the heart.

The animation, with its sequence of the progression, has stuck in my mind ever since I first saw it in 2017.

Looking back now—two years later, as I am writing this—I realize this was what I had *expected* of Alan's illness. But now I can see that his behavior was not following this road map. For him, the animated video was out of sequence.

Yes, the first region of the brain was impacted—the one involving short-term memory. But the second area? No, he wasn't losing words in his daily speech, and we could still play a short (because of attention span) game of Scrabble and he sometimes won. The third? No, his frontal region was still sharp. He could converse on many, if not all, subjects, even if he sometimes exaggerated or conflated facts or veered off topic. He was lucid.

What kind of predator was this, preying on my husband?

Over a few months, it was as if the animated video was on fast forward, skipping over regions and coming down hard on a different region of his brain, the occipital lobe, the region of vision.

The first time I noticed a new and alarming behavior was late summer of 2019, when we were driving a familiar residential street that we traveled several times a week.

"That looks like a tiger." Alan pointed. "A tiger on that lawn."

It was too soon for Halloween, when one might expect all manner of front yard decorations, monsters and ghouls and maybe a tiger. But this was an ordinary day in early autumn, and we were driving past blocks of neatly landscaped homes.

I didn't know what to say, so I joked about how Linus of the Peanuts cartoon strip imagined shapes in clouds. Alan responded with, "Something like that. It must have been a bush."

Soon there were other instances. He'd comment on how a fire hydrant looked like a person. It was almost childlike, the way he said it, but soon I realized this wasn't idle chatter. At home, around this same time, if I asked him to, say, carry something to the table, he began picking up the wrong object. At first I was annoyed, thinking that was just like a guy, not listening to me, ignoring my request. But it turned out that for my husband the connection between name and recognition of an object was slipping away.

"What is going on," I asked my Alzheimer's coach at the next support group meeting.

"It's a perceptual problem," she said. "Have you requested a PET scan?"

No, I had not, but a CT scan had been taken two years ago. That scan had shown some shrinkage of Alan's brain, but the analysis from the CT scan was nonspecific in terms of a dementia diagnosis. I had assumed the dementia was Alzheimer's, though I knew such a diagnosis could be elusive and at that time only determined conclusively by an autopsy.

"Ask your doctor for a PET scan," Audrey said. "You should do it soon."

At the next appointment with the neurologist, I described Alan's hallucinations, instances that my husband had more or less laughed off. This was not amusing to the physician, who ordered the scan.

From the moment we arrived at the appointment, it was apparent that a PET is serious business, both because it involves nuclear medicine and it is costly. The device I saw was small but intimidating. In order to block radioactive exposure, it was stored in a closed, lead-lined box.

Before we proceeded into a secure room, I had to sign an agreement that if Medicare and our supplemental insurance did not cover the cost of the scan then I would be responsible for a cost of about one thousand dollars. At this point, I figured if it helped me pin down my husband's dementia and provided some idea of the pathway ahead, I was ready to take the financial hit. Later it turned out our insurance did cover the test.

When the results came in, the first part of the summary read like this:

> Marked decrease in activity in the temporal lobes. Of concern is fairly marked occipital decreased activity. This is highly suggestive of Lewy body disease.

I knew this was the type of dementia made infamous by the death of actor Robin Williams. According to his wife, the effects of Lewy body with the hallucinations and the paranoia were why actor Robin Williams had taken his own life.

So it was Lewy bodies, more than plaques and tangles, that were attacking the regions of my husband's brain. But he was still articulate, seemingly highly cognitive. This is why the second part of the summary read: Slightly atypical of Lewy body disease is that there is normal activity in the frontal region.

Yes, at times he had been uncanny in problem solving, especially when it came to rebelling against imposed limitations. Did I feel thrown back to the uncertainty of that first verbal test at Hoag Neurological Institute in 2017? No. Because I now understood that dementia is a shape-shifter. I also understood the importance of community support.

From the beginning, I have never felt alone on this journey, even though Alan has continued to withdraw from me and I deeply miss my life partner. I have been, and continue to be, supported by his daughter, by the Alzheimer's community, and by the good fortune of finding a sensitive and excellent helper in Ryan. For all the anguish involved, I try to remind myself that I am a lucky caregiver spouse.

I also think my luck is partly a byproduct of reaching out.

Looking back, my own caregiver's journey began with the aid of three, one-hour sessions at Hoag, the clinic where we had the inexpensive memory assessment. The three follow-up sessions were offered at no cost. These combined information about dementia with my first experience of a support group, and I soon saw the benefit of asking questions, sharing experiences, and passing the tissues.

After completing the three Hoag sessions, I looked up the Alzheimer's Association in my county, and discovered that it, too, offered a series of classes and free, sponsored support groups around our county. I signed up for the classes, and after completing them, I tried two different support groups that met in local community centers. The second one I visited felt like a good fit for me. It has been my mainstay ever since.

Fast forward a few years. After receiving the PET scan results, I also began participating in a monthly, specialized support group for the families of patients with Lewy body and frontotemporal dementia. This group is also sponsored by the Alzheimer's Association. For me, this was mainly supplemental because many of the regulars at the general Alzheimer's group had become friends by that time, and still are to this day. They're my fellow travelers on this journey, and our guide, the group leader, is well versed in all aspects of dementia. As must be obvious by now, I consider participating in a support group as one of the keys to sanity and survival when your spouse, or any family member, has dementia.

I empathize with those who join our group, seeking a definitive diagnosis, hoping for clarity. Pinning down a diagnosis is a such a difficult matter, but I believe it makes sense to go forth by assuming that your mate's memory loss and other symptoms point to Alzheimer's. Then let time, emerging behavior, changes in the brain, and advances in medical technology sort it out. It can take months or years to determine the specific type of dementia. Had we taken a PET scan early on, I don't know if it would have pinpointed Alan's Lewy body dementia before it progressed.

After the PET scan and result in early fall of 2019, Alan's perceptual grasp on the world further slipped away. It began with paranoid questions about who was in the house.

"Are those people still here?" he might ask, or "Has she left yet?" But no one had been visiting at the house. This symptom, I learned, is known as "phantom boarders."

It progressed to his sometimes not recognizing me. Though I know the Alzheimer's rule is don't argue, yet on occasion—and especially when your mate, like mine, still has a largely intact frontal region—it is hard not to try to set the record straight. Especially when you have handy documents.

Then, in my presence, he began talking about me in the third person ... about Allene this and Allene that. If I countered with "Hi, it's me—Allene," he'd say, "I don't know who you are, but you are not Allene."

I would show him my photo ID. That worked for a while.

In one instance he asked, "Didn't we meet a couple of months ago?"

I know I should have changed the subject or walked away, but I had documents! I said, "Well, actually, we're married. We've been married for twenty-three years."

"That's not possible," he said. "I am not married."

I brought out our marriage certificate. More than once.

Bedtime seems to be a florid time for hallucinations, perhaps related to what's known as sundowner syndrome. One night, he came into our bedroom where I was reading and said, "I don't know who you are. Maybe one of the sisters." The sisters, I knew, were his aunts. They had passed on decades ago.

I was becoming a stranger to my husband. How long would it be before I was perceived as a threat to him? As an intruder? And if that happened, would he become a threat to me?

Remember Their Greatness

As a DEMENTIA CARER or caregiver frequently verging on melt-down, I have trouble following the admonition to remember their greatness. This recognition comes to me at unexpected moments.

It is late morning, and Alan is standing inside the open door of my home office, where I am clattering away on my laptop. He says, in a voice not suggesting alarm, "When you have a minute, I'd like help with something spooky."

"Spooky?"

I stop what I'm doing and follow him down the hallway to what he calls his office. This home was built when such an extension off the kitchen would have been called a breakfast room. Framed award plaques, certificates, and photographs dot the three walls of his alcove office, as if comprising a biography of his dual career and his volunteer work in retirement.

Now he has stopped in front of an object mounted in a small black frame with no glass. It is made of strings arranged on a fabric-covered board and is tactile, you can touch it.

He devised this teaching aid a few years ago when he volunteered to teach math to visually impaired students. Like many of the things hanging on the wall, it reflects his outreach over the years, the ways he helped others. But this is not what he remembers now. Instead, he tells me, "My mother brought this here." He is grieving, tears rimming his eyes.

But his mother died decades ago. She never set foot in this house, and she obviously has nothing to do with this memento on the wall. I risk causing further anguish by setting him straight, but I want him to know how much he was appreciated as a professor and a tutor. "The object in that frame," I tell him, "is from the time when you were teaching math and you also tutored blind students. You made that model to show them a particular math problem. So they could feel it."

"It seemed to help," he said.

Such relief! I have pulled him back to the present.

But then he asks, "Where did I teach?"

"Cal State Fullerton."

"Where?"

I repeat the answer and point to another framed object, Faculty Member of the Year.

"How is that possible?" he asks. "When was that?"

"Well ..." and I know I am entering sketchy territory here, trying to explain a sequence of events, "you retired early as an engineer and took up teaching math." I point out the framed Retirement Lunch photograph.

He suddenly leaves the breakfast room-office and begins walking around the house, pointing at art hanging on the walls in other rooms, art we purchased together, and attributing them to his mother ("She brought that here") or not recognizing them at all ("Where did that come from"). He seems to be trying to place these items in some kind of scrambled time-space framework in his mind.

After a loop through the hallway, he stops at a world map on the wall in the service porch. It bristles with blue and green push pins showing our journeys to different countries, blue for where we've been, green for where we still plan to go. Our trips. "I brought that," he says, "from my mother's place years ago."

The us of our married life begins to disappear.

Because it worked a few minutes ago, I try to summon reality again in the hope that his love of travel might change the channel. "Those are all the places we have gone together. See the pins on the map?"

"Together? I went with you?" He begins eyeing me suspiciously, and I morph from myself into you, a stranger. This isn't going well. Our home is a minefield of memorabilia that disorient and confuse him, that make him distraught. So many objects, in part because he has a habit of keeping just about everything. These mementos are no longer heart-warming but more like chilling *memento mori*, reminders of death. I must end this woeful tour around the house.

Maybe a drive, I think, but then I remember how this used to redirect him but no longer does so. Visual delusions and hallucinations of people appear, as if a projection screen has replaced the windshield, as if a hologram display floats in the back seat. If we went for a drive, I'd hear him say, "Who is that, out there? Who else is in the car? Who are all these people?"

No, I will redirect him outdoors, on foot.

By this time, it is almost noon, when the caterpillars are warm and most active. Alan is immediately engaged. The first thing we see on the wooden trellis by the side door and as if right on cue, is a dangling caterpillar transformed minutes ago into the pre-pupa, upside-down-J position. They don't all make it to this advanced phase, and this one looks healthy, plump and promising. We find two more big caterpillars foraging and basking in the sun.

Back in a safe mental zone, we peer into the leaves and find another one, a toddler caterpillar of pale yellow with tiny thin stripes.

"That's three cats and a J," I say. "Hooray!"

"I second that," he says. "Hooray!"

It is nearing the end of the milkweed season. Soon I will have to cut back the stems to a nub so the plants will regenerate for the coming year. But for now, I am grateful for the joyful distraction of our summer visitors. Dementia, it seems to me, goes down better with butterflies.

Chapter 7
AUTUMN SHADOWS

The Perfect Storm

IT'S A CLICHÉ, I know, but a perfect storm crashed down on me in November of 2019. No one expects a convergence of wind, current, and tidal bore until it hits. Only later, much later, would I call it a gift.

I'd had my annual mammogram with no reason to suspect anything amiss, then while standing at the checkout counter in a drug store, of all places, I answered a call on my mobile. "The 3-D mammogram showed a disturbance in the right breast," the voice told me. "You will need to schedule a needle biopsy."

That would be a first for me, but of course I complied and arranged for the procedure. Splayed face down with your face in a hole makes for an uncomfortable procedure, and worse comes when the needle hits its mark. Still, I felt hopeful. Friends of mine had gone this far only to learn it was a false alarm, so I thought I'd probably dodge big trouble. Not that I needed more trouble.

On the Tuesday before Thanksgiving, I received the second call: the biopsy showed a tumor. I felt a whirl of vertigo, the time-stopping knowledge that my life had just changed, again, but this time it wasn't my husband who was the patient. This wasn't about Lewy bodies or plaques and tangles. Now my own cells had turned against me.

Tuesdays were also one of my precious, weekly, caregiver-covered afternoons, and when that second call came, I happened to be on my way to meet Michiko, one of my oldest friends. We had a date to partake in our longstanding tradition of catching up over coffee and pie.

Continuing on my way to meet Michiko, I was beset by dark thoughts. Why me? Why now, when Alan's condition is deteriorating daily? How could I keep a safe eye on him during the complicated process I was facing, during a frightening journey into the medical labyrinth?

But isn't *why me?* what anyone asks when they learn they have cancer?

On the day of the needle biopsy, before the device was inserted and just in case, I had tried to make a deal with whatever deity might be listening: Please spare me so I can take care of my husband—who barely knows who I am, who calls me Mom or Aunt Mary or confuses me with a former girlfriend, who thinks the house is full of phantom boarders, who keeps stuffing the house and car with tools and debris from the garage, who is unaware of where he is on any given day. Chicago? Southern California?

Please spare me. I tried to bargain. Or, I asked, at least wait. But no deal.

I had not been granted a reprieve, so now that I wasn't to be spared the surgery and probably not the cycle of radiation treatments either, I tried to envision a bright horizon past recovery, me strong again and ready for the challenge of caring for my husband. I just couldn't see it. I felt helpless, and all I saw ahead were darkness and chaos.

Which is what I told my friend when I arrived at the cafe where we'd met for years. There I sat at the best-in-town pie café, and across from me, Michiko, a retired teacher I have known since our middle school days. Before us sat slices of lemon cream and boysenberry pie, mine untouched, fat tears rolling down my face, because it is true, as they say ... first you cry.

Thanksgiving was at hand. What was I thankful for? Besides, holidays suck when it comes to arranging appointments for medical treatment. From across the table, Michiko cast me tender and encouraging looks as I worked my iPhone and tried to pin down copies of my test results to hand-carry from one health care system in Long Beach, where I'd had the needed biopsy, to a clinic twenty miles away and closer to my house. It had to be closer because I'd need to manage Alan throughout whatever procedure lay ahead. I wanted to get this behind me before he became worse, and he was becoming worse day by day.

I never talk on the phone in a restaurant. I think it's rude and distracting to others. But this day I didn't care. I was in a selfish survival mode, making calls, climbing phone trees, waiting frozen on hold, toughing out transfers between departments. At one point, I was on my iPhone with a lab, and Michiko was on her mobile seeking the contact number I needed for another clinic. It took our four hands on two iPhones and the luck of reaching a sympathetic lab tech who said she'd override the standard three days and do her best to expedite the slide I needed.

The next day—the Wednesday before Thanksgiving—the lab tech came through, and thanks to my friend's help with phone contacts, I was able to grab an appointment (a cancellation) at a busy breast clinic the following week.

There would be much shuttling around in the days ahead. A consultation with a breast surgeon. MRI and blood work. Picking up CDs and slides and hand carrying them for expediency in pinning down further appointments. All this frantic activity was punctuated by car rides with Alan as my mandatory sidekick as he kept asking questions. "Who is driving this car?" "Is my mother still alive?" "Where does our money come from?" "Where am I?" "Do I know you?"

Not surprisingly my blood pressure, usually on the low side, climbed.

Now I'll take a breath and give you a breather too, because the pieces fell into place between Thanksgiving and Christmas. I consulted with two different surgeons, both highly recommended, but I liked the second one better. I felt an affinity for her, and isn't human connection the most precious of gifts?

Once I had decided on a surgeon and settled into numb and trusting submission, I fairly sleepwalked through the next round of appointments. That is, until at one of these Alan's behavior revealed that we had entered another phase of his illness.

It happened to be the day before Christmas Eve, when I had a consultation with a radiation oncologist. Stretches of daily radiation had been one of my greatest concerns. What would I do with Alan while I was tied up? Ever since his dementia had become apparent, he'd often come with me to my routine appointments. Well, no longer. Hallucinations made his behavior disturbing, and sometimes he refused to leave the house and come with me.

On the day I saw this radiologist, because it was not a caregiver Tuesday or Saturday, I had no choice but to bring Alan along. True, he brought one of his books to read, and I was grateful that even if he read the same page over and over it still seemed to engage him. We sat in the waiting room for what seemed a long time. Then my name was finally called. I rose from the chair, only to hear my husband say, "I think I'll walk home."

Walk home? My brain nearly short-circuited as I tossed overboard every Alzheimer's rule and lost any modicum of cool I had left. "*Walk home? Nooo*," I hissed, turning heads. "You will get lost. You must stay here in the waiting room. Please. I am sick. I have cancer. I need, need, need your cooperation!"

"Well ... okay," he said. I was unconvinced that he meant it.

I headed into the examination room and my meeting with the radiologist. While I sat in there, awaiting his arrival, I thought about what Alan had said, about how the chance of his wandering away was sure to escalate from this day forward.

Magnifying that day's worry, the radiation oncologist was delayed. My total appointment time stretched to two and a half hours, at the end of which I expected to find my husband gone. If so, I figured I'd activate the Find My Friend app and hope to track him via geo-location, thanks to the iPhone in his belt holster.

But I found him still glued to his chair in the waiting room. Looking distraught.

"What's wrong?" I asked.

"Some people accosted me," he said, his forehead scrunched with anger. "They mugged me and took my wristwatch and wallet." But I could see his wristwatch was still on his arm, and when I asked him to please stand up so we could go home, I saw his wallet was still snug in its usual place in his back pocket.

Only when we got home would I process this latest discouraging development—the threat of wandering compounded by paranoia. There are moments when we're dealing with a loved one with dementia when the next step becomes clear, and this was such a time. Alan could no longer accompany me to any place where he would be out of my sight. Another shoe fell. Another big thud.

Yet here I was on a path of treatment. In order to show up at my own multiple appointments I'd need a wrap-around strategy, a veritable Chernobyl dome of containment for my toxic-though-not-his-fault husband.

One approach would be to try to enroll him in senior day care for dementia patients, which might yield many consistent days of outside caregiving. Another approach would be to increase home caregiver coverage. But I'd already found it can be difficult to schedule a caregiver exactly when you need him or her, such as appointments. Maybe I'd cobble together a combination.

Yes, Alan would loudly object to everything I suggested or tried, but now I had leverage. I would play the cancer card.

I decided I would make my case as if I were presenting a shocking snapshot of his behavior on December 23. I knew this would break caregiver rules by my reminding him of how he had threatened to walk away. How it had sent my blood pressure soaring. How he had claimed he was mugged, but he wasn't. Rubbing his face in his bad behavior, as if saying "bad dog," was a radical breach of dementia caregiver rules. But I didn't care. My own life was now at stake.

I knew the many days of external beam radiation after surgery might serve my other challenge, which was to start conditioning Alan as we moved toward his eventual placement in a memory care facility. It was becoming clear that at some point, and especially with the Lewy body diagnosis, he would need full-time professional care, the kind I could not give him much longer at home.

And I now had a credible justification for daycare. It would psychologically prepare him to spend time with other impaired seniors and to accept the presence of a changing staff of caregivers.

When it came to my radiation treatment excuse and starting his daycare—even if I had to repeatedly intone, even shriek, *Breast cancer. Remember I have breast cancer!*—he could no longer say no.

Under the Tree

FOR ABOUT A YEAR, I had lived with the fading but still chilling possibility that Alan might take his life with a leap from a high branch of our huge ash tree. I had come up with a redirection by diverting his attention to a different ending to our story: a shared niche in a beautiful mosaic wall overlooking a memorial garden.

I wouldn't know if this ultimate workaround had succeeded until sometime in the future, at the end of his dementia journey. I hoped that would be a gentle ending, and that a plunge from the ash tree wouldn't be the image I would carry with me for the rest of my days.

Since we'd signed the cemetery agreement, he seemed to ignore the tree entirely. As a precaution, however, I changed the lock on the tree house hatch. I figured that if he ever was motivated to jump and the lock didn't open and he was faced with a delay, maybe he would just forget and walk away.

Then along came the cusp of 2019-2020, when his daughter Cathy scheduled a week's visit to spend time with her father between Christmas and New Year's. We were already in a semi-crisis mode. A month later, she would be flying out from Chicago again to help during my recovery from surgery.

Alan had not mentioned the tree house lately, so I thought my mosaic-wall plan had solved the problem. Then, at one point during Cathy's holiday visit when she and I were chatting, I looked through the window and saw that he was on the move.

He was climbing the wooden ladder up to the tree house.

"Oh, God," I said. "He hasn't been up there in months. I thought he'd forgotten about it!" Cathy and I looked at each other. She knew I'd changed the lock on the hatch, and he was about to find that the old key in the collection on his keyring didn't work.

"We'd better try to stop him," I said.

With dementia, and especially a tendency toward Lewy body dementia, a major issue is balance. He had already fallen recently while crossing the street, and again in the garage, both falls causing minor injuries and requiring a trip to urgent care in one case and to an orthopedist the second time. But he'd forgotten about those falls, and no one could convince him that he wasn't as agile and athletic as ever.

With my surgery coming up, the last thing we needed was for him to break his leg, so we headed out the front door, intent on talking him down. Because he has always listened to his daughter more than to me, she took point. "Dad, please come down! You might get hurt."

"Get hurt?" he bellowed. "It's my tree house. I built it. You are speaking to someone who has made thousands of successful skydives."

His skydiving statement was an exaggeration, but that wasn't my concern. What was my worry was the object I saw gripped in his hand. He was holding a bolt cutter. When he had recently lost the key to a backyard shed, he'd used a bolt cutter on the lock. But when it snapped through the metal, the kickback had knocked him off his feet and smack onto a brick planter. He'd ended up at urgent care with a painful shoulder and lacerations.

Now he was about to cut off another lock. This time, if he succeeded, it would be a major feat. It required no-hands balance atop a ladder while also managing the tension release that comes with the sudden snap of the bolt cutter through the metal lock. It would be a nearly impossible task, even for someone not afflicted with dementia.

As he positioned the tool, we called out simultaneously, "No, Dad!" and "No, Alan!" "You can't safely hold onto the ladder and cut the bolt, too," I added.

Glowering, he called down, "Watch me. I've survived a thousand skydives, and you can't make me stop what I'm doing."

We called up to him again, entreating him to come down, but, outraged by the two of us trying to thwart him, he yelled, "You people are trying to take me to federal prison!"

It was clear that he had no idea who we were.

"Wait," I said in desperation. "I think I have a copy of the key somewhere." This at least stopped him from using the bolt cutter.

While Cathy continued to hold his attention, I ran into the house, found the key I had hidden, then came back and handed it up to him. "Try this." And, of course, it fit. Luckily, he decided to climb down the ladder rather than continue up through the hatch. The bolt cutter crisis was over. What remained was the shock of seeing such hatred in his eyes.

"He didn't even know me," his only child said.

Cathy was seeing what I face every day when he doesn't know who I am. I was haltingly adapting to this process of a long goodbye. For his daughter, this was the man who had been her rock for a lifetime.

It shook me, of course, seeing her join me in the helpless space I had occupied for months. But later that day she adopted a different tone, one of resolve. "I was afraid of him," she said. "Before I come back for your surgery next month, I'd like you to install a lock on the guest room door. I have the kids to think about." I sensed what was coming because I felt it, too, when she added, "I don't want him mistaking me for an intruder."

When anger met paranoia in Alan's afflicted mind, it had morphed into his inability to recognize either of us. Then she asked me, "Do you feel safe sleeping in the same room with him at night?"

I thought about this for a minute. So far, his hallucinations had occurred mainly by day or in the angled light of a reading lamp. Strangely enough, I still felt secure with him in the dark, when his hand always touched me as he slept next to me. Usually, he slid a few fingers under my hip as I slept on my side, or sometimes he gently pressed his hand against me, as if seeking reassurance that I was there, that he wasn't alone.

"I still feel fine with him at night," I replied, suddenly trying to convince myself. I didn't mention how not long ago he had brought an axe from the garage into the house and left it lying on the kitchen counter. But that was in the daytime, and on the day the axe showed up, though momentarily alarmed, I rationalized that this was another variant on his latest "job," which was the hauling of tools from the garage into the house, then taking them back again. And he had taken the axe back into the garage.

After the tree house incident, after he'd perceived us as his persecutors, that's when I became aware of a rising level of fear.

More precautions were needed. I already had a lock on my office door, a legacy of a previous owner. Soon I would install one on the guest room door. Either might need to double as a safe room.

Looking back as I write this at the end of January 2020, I can report that I was fortunate because the operation and post-surgery phase went surprisingly well. Cathy took family leave from work and stayed with us for a week. Our dependable Ryan added temporary extra days to his schedule.

The two of them managed my husband so I didn't need to chase after him or keep up with meals or laundry or countless other daily tasks. Having Alan's daughter here, and Ryan as a backup, was a blessing beyond words. How could I once have insisted that I didn't need help?

The post-op pain was less than I'd imagined, so I didn't even need pain meds. Once I was tucked in at home, I slept and slept. For the next two days, while wearing a cozy teal shawl Cathy bought for me, I read novels like a woman lounging on vacation. The following weekend, when it was time to remove the body-spanning, tube top bandage, I was relieved to see what lay beneath. Under its translucent bandage, my right breast had a small incision from the lumpectomy, but appeared mainly intact. "It might leave a little divot," my surgeon had said, referring to the resulting scar.

And it got better! When I heard the pathology results, I felt like I'd been handed a report card filled with A's at the end of a grueling term. Clear margins and lymph nodes. The tumor was smaller than anticipated, and of a type less likely to recur.

It seemed the perfect storm had moved on.

A Fountain of Leaves

YET EVEN as life became darker, there were bright moments still. The ash tree, that looming landmark in our front yard, was both a liability and an asset. A few weeks before my scheduled surgery, both aspects converged on a January day that began with despair and ended with celebration.

Every year, the holiday season coincides with a natural occurrence. Around the winter solstice, like calendar clockwork, thousands of leaves drop from the boughs of this huge tree. Usually, Alan arranged for major tree trimming in alternate years, but because of his affliction he had forgotten this year. It didn't occur to me to schedule tree service.

By the first week of January, the brown leaves had been drifting down for days, mounding like dunes. At first, I welcomed them because disposing of the leaves gave Alan a seasonal daily task, "one of my jobs." He seemed cheerful as he methodically swept up and reduced the accumulation. That is, until a further dip in temperature caused thousands more leaves to fall overnight.

The piles became more than he could handle, inducing a beyond-his-control panic. "I have to do something about this mess!" he said, tense with anxiety.

"Okay," I said. "I'll try to find a leaf removal service." But a Google search of that phrase didn't turn one up, at least not in our area of Southern California. I conveyed this news and offered to help him with the sweeping and raking and scooping-up but he sighed. "No, it's my job." He returned to his task like the mythical Sisyphus, who was punished by the gods and forced to push a massive boulder, which kept rolling down a hill, back up the hill for all eternity.

But a few minutes later, the gods gave us a break.

He came inside and told me that a woman and her little boy were standing in the front yard. "They want to know if it is okay if the boy rakes up our leaves," he said.

How was this possible? Sure, I'd been hoping for help, but I was picturing a couple of guys with a truck. A woman with a kid? This seemed like another instance of my husband's phantom boarders, and yet when I walked out to the front yard ... there they were, flesh and blood. The forty-something mom introduced herself as Erin, and we met her eight-year-old son, Kit. "He loves to rake leaves," she told us, "and he's already raked up all of ours. I'll help him," she added softly, "to keep an eye on things."

I was almost speechless. Finally, I said, "How amazing ... I was just trying to find a leaf removal service. We'd be glad to pay him whatever you think is fair."

"Free is fair," she said. "You'd be doing us a favor. But he would like to go up to the tree house, if that's okay. I'll take a photo. That's plenty of payment for us."

"Raking leaves is tiring work," I said. Then it dawned on me that maybe she was trying to keep her active, and maybe hyperactive, boy busy. Our lawn might serve as today's playground-therapy for both Kit and Alan, for her family and mine.

And so it turned into a party. We plunged in together by grabbing rakes (and borrowing a couple more from our neighbors) and rolling our big, green, waste disposal bin around the sidewalk into the best position for receiving leaves dumped in by the scoopful. When our bin became too full, we borrowed another one from next door. To further increase capacity, Alan and Erin held Kit by the arms while he jumped on the contents, compressing the mass enough to add more leaves.

The end result was a front lawn nearly as smooth as a golf course— well, except for the lumpy places over the ash tree's roots. Now it was time for Kit's payment, so I scrambled up the ladder and inserted the key for the hatch lock before Alan had a chance to see if his own key would fit. After I climbed down, Kit trailed Alan up the wooden ladder. The two of them clambered through the hatch, then stood at the railing, grinning, Alan like another kid. Both of them waved down to us.

I was struck by the contrast with the angry scene in the tree house less than two weeks ago. That was rage. This was joy.

Next came a couple clicks of Erin's iPhone, and Kit's mom had her picture. I wanted to pay him with cash but she still resisted. We worked it out, though, while the boy climbed back down the ladder and headed our way. "He more than earned this," I said, offering her four $10 bills. Eventually she and I agreed, and I gave him three.

All in all, we'd had a holiday-card winter afternoon. Also I had the grateful and almost vertical feeling of time suspended, knowing these were moments I would treasure always: Watching the boy squeal with delight, his mother laughing, Alan fully engaged and laughing, too ... my husband in motion at a time in his life when he had few chances to express himself physically or socially, revisiting his best self—athlete, engineer, and teacher, I silently repeated the Alzheimer's adage: Remember his greatness.

As we were returning rakes to the garage, Erin noticed our back yard orange tree, its branches groaning under ripe globes of fruit. I had worked hard to keep Alan, with his balance problems, off the tall ladder, so like the leaves, the unpicked oranges had accumulated. "Oh," she said, "I'd love to have some of those."

"We have more than we can eat," I told her. "Please, you'd do me a favor if you take some. Take lots. I'll bring out tote bags you can use and keep."

And so the day ended with another unexpected gift, a solution for disbursing our over-abundance of produce. We had shared the bounty and the workload of two trees with this woman and her son, who were not hallucinations, after all, but neighbors and now our new friends.

Chapter 8
DISGUISED GIFTS

Like a Glove

I KNEW THE DAY WAS FAST APPROACHING when Alan would need to be placed in a memory care facility. One of my criteria had already been met: for stretches of time he didn't know me. Except then he knew me again. It was like the queasy motion of a three-axle thrill ride without the fun. At that point, in early February of 2020, he was at least cooperating by attending specialized adult day care for half a day each week. I had played the cancer card, and he had bought into my excuse of needing weekly oncology appointments.

Americana, the private daycare facility for dementia patients, was bright and cheerful, with capable young caregivers who managed activities and a chef who served excellent meals. Once again, the prospect of good food helped smooth the way. I hoped the experience of half a day a week would prepare him for future placement.

But I was not ready for that. I needed greater certainty. I didn't know that my second criterion was about to be met.

Then, too, I had no inkling that within a month—when certainty about placement finally arrived—it would collide with a global pandemic. We didn't know we would soon be living in a world of masks with looping televised news cycles showing teams of nurses and doctors swaddled in protective gowns and gloves. Shortly before the pandemic hit, Alan and I had our own run-in with gloves.

I'd been struggling to maintain a weekly routine, and part of that routine involved the garage. It continued to function as his Man Cave, a sandbox, his playground, where he found count-less opportunities for arranging and moving and rearranging and hanging all sorts of things on hooks; or coiling and uncoiling hoses and chains and tubes; or propping up brooms and rakes and different sized loppers and nippers for trimming the branches of fruit trees. I was glad his fiddling in the garage occupied him for many daylight hours.

On half-Tuesdays and Thursdays and Saturdays, Ryan would hang out in the garage with him. On other days, if I kept an eye out (to be sure my husband wasn't, say, climbing a ladder), then he seemed fine in the garage by himself.

Except all this messing around with metal and wood in arid winter weather was leaving his hands dry and cracked, and one day he ended up with an angry looking cut verging on an infec-tion. After another trip to urgent care, where I explained how the cut had happened, and after cleaning and application of unguents and gauze, the doctor said, "You must wear gloves if you are working in the garage."

Needing a tangible reminder, I asked the physician "Would you please write that on a prescription pad?" He did so, with all the formality lent by the clinic's logo printed on the top of each page. It read: 1) wear gloves; 2) apply lotion twice a day.

Silly me, to think that this mandate by an authority in a white coat would guarantee Alan's compliance, not when resistance was one of his last bastions of freedom. He would always exert his will when I, despite having his health and safety foremost in mind, told him what not to do or what to do … in this case, wearing protective gloves, and applying lotion twice a day.

He'd seemed agreeable enough in the doctor's office, but once we arrived home, he headed straight for the garage, and when I held out the gloves, he said, "No, I won't wear them!"

However gently I coaxed, it was, "Don't want to!"

No matter if I showed him the doctor's clearly written order, no matter if his hands hurt, if they bled and I repeatedly applied an antiseptic and unguents and bandages, he still refused. What could I do? Not much, it turned out. Except turn to Ryan.

When he was on duty during those winter days, the two of them spent his caregiver's shift in the garage. Call it man to man, which didn't apply to me. And being engaged in the Man Cave, Ryan could casually drop in the request, maybe with an offhand remark like, "Hey, Al, why don't you slip on these gloves?" Being already engaged with his buddy, Alan would comply. Or, as Ryan explained to me, "When you walk out of the house and into the garage, he refuses the gloves because he perceives you as coming at him. I am with him already, so when I ask him, it seems natural."

But our caregiver wasn't with him every day, and his current schedule didn't allow him to add additional weekly time with Alan. That left many hours (less the one-half day at daycare) of my saying, "Would you please wear these gloves," to which the answer was always "No!" spiking my worry about more trips to urgent care or, worse, a serious infection.

Then I thought, Maybe I am wrong here.

Would a better wife choose to spend those long and chilling daylight hours hanging out in the garage, like Ryan does? Could I muster the discipline to do it, the way my sixteen-year-old self once hung out with a high school boyfriend while he earned spending money by working in a gas station on weekends? Well, I couldn't picture the adult me in the Man Cave, day after day. It was a tedious prospect with an unknown timeline of months or years... because, I thought, This is my life, too.

But constant guilt is unavoidable in a marriage to a dementia patient, so I kept thinking, Well, if I could keep gas-station company with a high school boyfriend, then couldn't I do this for my husband, when it really counts? Couldn't I hang out and keep watch for hours, occasionally saying, as Ryan does, "Hey, Al, how about slipping on these gloves?" even if I was likely to go crazy with boredom.

Then I woke out of a snooze-alarm dream one morning and knew I had a solution, a project with a purpose. It dawned on me that someday in the future I would need to give away or sell or donate or otherwise liquidate the brimming contents of this garage.

I had no idea what many of the items in his engineer's jumble of a Man Cave were even used for.

So I decided to help him organize, sort out the mess of tools and gadgets that were dangling, strewn, and stacked everywhere in no particular order. Adding to the problem of layers like an archaeological dig was the wrinkle that in recent years he had taken to purchasing duplicates in hardware stores or online when he could no longer remember where the originals were located, or even if he already owned one.

He said he liked my organizing idea. But neither of us knew the project was about to turn up duplicates, triplicates and quadruplicates. Who needs four axes?

After I started hanging out, which he seemed to enjoy, we got into a rhythm. "What's this thing for?" I'd ask. He would dip into his long-term memory to retrieve an impersonal fact, and he always came up with an answer.

Then I would come back with a stab at a category. "Oh," I might say, "then could you call this thing a type of Measurement Device?" And if I'd guessed correctly, he'd reply, "Yes, that describes it" and I'd hear a hint of approval in his voice.

With a term pinned down, I would make a label with a Sharpie on an index card and tape it on the workbench or on a shelf or anywhere we had surface space to gather similarly sorted objects. We organized by category this way, and soon the garage began shaping up.

To my surprise, my work with him was not a sacrificial time of boredom and tedium as if I felt my life wasting away. No, not at all. Instead, it became many hours of unexpected sweetness.

Despite my being surrounded by metal and plastic and tubes and screws and wood and greasy things I'd never appreciated, we were in a kind of flow, working as a team. This period spent with my husband would join the caterpillars and the day of the fountain of leaves in my virtual scrapbook of how some days still felt like the best of times.

I had to store up my memories of those cherished hours because they didn't last long.

Too soon, it became evident that perils lurked inside the Man Cave. One morning, convinced I was not his wife but an impostor, Alan accused me of stealing from him. This paranoia escalated, and at one point for no apparent reason, he held up a metal rod and growled, "Get out of the garage."

Two years earlier I had removed the guns from the house. More recently, I had hidden the large kitchen knives and other sharp kitchen implements. Just in case. Now the time had come to hide certain tools. But I was running out of secure hideaway space in the house, so when I had a chance, I quietly slipped the axes and a few other potentially lethal objects under blankets in the trunk of the car. During my next Ryan-covered day, I rented a storage unit.

As with many dementia-related detours, the greater problem of a garage containing far too many pointy and sharp metal objects couldn't be solved until a ripe moment arose. I needed a chance to take a more decisive step. This happened the day he forgot the sequence for the garage door opener.

"What's the code?" he asked.

"Oh, I'll take care of it," I said with false gaiety, and then I punched in the code while standing at an angle that blocked him from seeing the finger pattern. It was a number he had long used for many passwords, his daughter's birthday. This marked the first time he had forgotten it and he would never remember again.

From that day forward, it was a small step to telling him a loving lie so he didn't even try to remember the number sequence. "The garage door opener is broken," I explained a few days later, "and the repairman is out of town." The garage, the former Man Cave, would remain closed for business until after my waffling about his future was over, until I knew it was time for placement. Until I had reached certainty beyond a doubt.

Finding Certainty

WHAT NEXT TIPPED me toward the big decision was, of all things, shopping for groceries.

As of mid-February of 2020, I was still relying on our weekly excursion to Albertsons, which, as I've mentioned, has a Starbucks with little tables and chairs for him to wait while I'm shopping, then after I'd paid, he'd help me wheel out the groceries and load them into the car.

Despite the stress of our life, simply entering the familiar layout of the store had taken on the feeling for me of coming home. Once inside the entrance, I'd walk past the colorful and fragrant floral department and take a deep breath. The familiar aisles and signage gave me a feeling of being grounded. For a few minutes as I was finding the products and produce on my list, I was in the Shopping Zone.

I could keep an eye on him too, because when I reached the front end-cap of an aisle, he'd be in view at the Starbucks table. I'd try to catch his eye and wave.

Then one morning as we arrived, he told me he was heading to the men's room, located in the front of the store. I said, "I'll order our coffee and leave yours on the side table where you can add the sweetener."

I didn't think much about it. I ordered the coffee, left his as agreed, set mine in the cart's cup holder, and set about shopping. After navigating one aisle, I reached the front and glanced over, expecting to see him at the little table by now. No Alan. *That's odd*, I thought.

Leaving my cart behind, I went to investigate, heading first for the single-user men's room where I saw a man exit, so I knew my husband wasn't inside. Then I noticed how one of the store's exterior doors was only a few steps away... *Oh no*, I thought, but oh yes, he had kept right on walking, right out the exterior door, across the large parking lot, and toward a major intersection. That's where I found him, poised to cross a busy four-lane street.

This moment marked the beginning of what Ryan called "his ambulation." This is a compulsion in a patient with dementia to walk, to flee, to seek an exit, to head for an unknown destination *out there somewhere.*

It had been a while since two previous, but widely spaced, incidents of walking away, but those were different. The first had been about a year ago, when he'd headed on foot for our bank, became turned around and didn't find it, but managed to find his way home. The second time, more recently, he'd explained he "just wanted to go for a walk in the neighborhood," but he got lost among residential streets where he'd lived for almost three decades. I drove around until I found him a few blocks away. He seemed to understand that his stroll hadn't been a good idea, and a couple of weeks had passed without incident.

This current ambulation, this walkabout away from the grocery store, marked the beginning of a new phase. When *wandering* becomes *fleeing*, you know your loved one is at serious risk.

The immediate solution was to keep him with me in the store. The next time I said, "It would be so helpful if you'd push the cart for me. And keep an eye on my purse," I added, "if I have to look for something, maybe an aisle away." He agreed. Our lattes were nested in the cart's cup holders, and he pushed the cart while I shopped.

But this new routine coincided with the emergence of another new phase, the ramping up of his hallucinations. He had experienced many hallucinations by this time. Sometimes he acknowledged them with an awareness that the real was somehow mixed up with the imaginary. It was more alarming to me, however, when his delusions were populated with people from his past.

One day as we rolled down the aisle in Albertsons, he said, "I just saw Jennifer," referring to a former, long-time girlfriend. "She's right over there." He pointed. It wasn't a case of mistaken identity, because no one was standing there at all.

The next time we were in the store he saw her again. As we walked down an aisle toward buying a bag of his favorite Mini Crunch chocolate bars, which he had begun consuming daily by the dozen, he said, "Jen is here." Again, no Jen.

I'd tried to avoid disagreeing with him about delusions and obey dementia-caregiver rule No. 1 of Don't argue. True, I'd had trouble following the don't-debate-them rule when he'd seemed so high functioning, but this was a new type of delusion, a series of visions, his belief that an ex-girlfriend frequented the supermarket and was following us around like a wraith.

By the next week, he seemed to have taken the matter in hand. He told me he no longer wanted to go shopping with me. "It upsets me too much to see people in the store," he explained, his implied phrase being *people who are not there.* I soon shifted my weekly pantry-stocking trip to my Ryan-covered days, and I went to the store alone.

Circumstances changed again soon after this. A new catch phase started in the middle of the night when a distressed Alan woke me, saying, "Who *are* you?"

I turned on the bedside light. "It's me, Allene. I'm your wife."

"Not possible. I don't have a wife. Where is this place?"

"Your house. Our house."

"You and your people are trying to *swindle* me."

I saw fear in his eyes and my heart clenched in my chest. "Uh oh," I said. "I have a headache. I think it's best if I sleep in the guest room."

Which I did. And I locked the door.

A day or so later, when Ryan arrives but before I set out on my errands—only to essential destinations at this point—I update him. First, because we are worried about the problem of fleeing, I tell

Ryan that Alan had removed his Medic Alert that morning. Worn on a chain around his neck, it shows his name, my phone contact, and dementia as a medical condition, also his allergy. He has worn a Medic Alert in one version or other since the Army determined that he was allergic to penicillin. "I convinced him to put it back on," I told Ryan.

Second, my husband was lately into chemicals. He had somehow modified a dispenser of hand soap I keep on the kitchen sink. It was ordinarily filled with pearly white liquid, but now the contents of the dispenser had turned brown "I can't imagine what he added to change the color of that soap," I said, and then I went on with a list of other things that had happened since Ryan was here a couple of days ago: "I also found Lysol toilet bowl cleaner in the refrigerator, and he'd opened a container of dishwashing pods and put them in the fridge too."

"Be careful," Ryan said. "He might start adulterating the food you use for cooking."

And there was more. "Alan started turning on the gas stove," I said, "so I removed the knobs. Now it's no knives, no knobs. The kitchen is disabled." My voice scaled higher in my distress.

Ryan could see my state. "You know ..." he said softly, "you won't have to do this much longer."

I knew that when Ryan's words came true, I would face a heavy price in guilt. Did it seem possible that just three years ago, even as recently as a few months ago, I had imagined it was possible for me to care for Alan at home?

Ever since I had first explored the prospect of placing him in a memory care facility, I had prayed that—if the time came—Alan would be so clearly ready that I would not hesitate.

I'd had two criteria. One was if he did not know me and thought I was a stranger. The other was if he was angry and paranoid. Now there was even the remote chance, however accidental, of poisoning both of us. The time had arrived. I was certain.

The Actor and Her Calendar

THIS IS FEBRUARY 18, 2020, three days after our twenty-third anniversary, which passed without acknowledgment. I didn't mention it to my husband to avoid triggering his usual protest that we are not married. Since our first date in 1992, this is the first time we haven't celebrated at our lovely Indian restaurant. We always took our engraved silver anniversary cups for a champagne toast, and the restaurant would fast-chill them.

But not this year.

Now I am looking at the calendar for a different reason. This date marks two kinds of countdowns.

One involves the loving lies essential for a caregiver's survival, in order to help ensure that she does not expire before her dementia-afflicted spouse.

Today I will draft a plan for a fictional radiation schedule, even though I will not be undergoing radiation. In other words, this will be a play-the-cancer-card calendar. I'll need to become an actor for the next several weeks. Unknown to Alan, my end goal will be a specific date for him to enter a memory care residence.

Another goal of the fake calendar is to induce Alan to spend more time in senior daycare during my supposed three-week radiation treatment schedule.

For this, I will need to be definite, calendar-confident, when I say I have an appointment for treatment. It is my hope that his current resistance to spending time with other afflicted seniors will diminish, that in his heart of hearts he will gradually come to understand that he is one of them.

So now I am in the public library, this being one of Ryan's coverage days. Even better for my concentration, I am in a private study room I have reserved. I've brought a wall calendar as well as my laptop, and I am hoping that drafting a strategy and writing it out will help me clear my head.

I have said that today marks two kinds of countdowns, one being the fictional treatment calendar.

The other is to wean Alan off one set of meds so he can begin a different regimen.

At my Alzheimer's support group, talk of meds always comes up, always fills part of the discussion, though everyone defers to physicians. Discussing prescription meds is not, after all, like suggesting vitamins or supplements.

In our case, my husband began this journey under a psychiatrist's care with a specific anti-depressant. A few months later, when his memory loss became more severe, we knew we had a dementia issue but still thought the antidepressants were helpful.

As a result, he has been taking them ever since.

As his dementia progressed, the lead doctor became his neurologist, who has his own protocol for his patients, depending on the type of dementia.

But before the neurologist would be willing to sign off on Alan's transition to a memory care facility—which requires the signature of two physicians, the other being our primary care physician—we've had to gradually wean Alan off his current antidepressant. The neurologist gave us a step-down in dosage, and this has been under way for the past four weeks.

The last phase of the lowest dosage starts today and continues for two more weeks. That will bring us to March 3.

I know what comes after that, and I dread it.

I will need to persuade my husband to voluntarily walk into a memory care facility, the one that his daughter and I have selected. This involves a lie, a ploy, a big deception—there's no other way to say it. I've been told about a time-tested way to pull it off. The "transition" goes like this:

On the appointed day, I will bring him to the facility to meet Ryan for lunch, supposedly to see the "nice other place" where Ryan works when he is not with us. We will be served a prearranged lunch in one of the small, private dining areas, a gourmet meal including a glass of wine. Then, as the script goes, I will excuse myself to go to the restroom ... and I will not come back.

Ryan, who will remain at the table with Alan, will give him the excuse I have crafted: "Allene needs another surgery, and while she recovers you'll be staying here for a while."

He will next help Alan get settled in his room, which will be set up in advance with changes of clothes and some of his other personal things. I've been told that only after a few days of adjustment would it be wise for me to return to the facility and visit him.

And that is how it is supposed to go.

Chapter 9
CHRYSALIS

A Virus Eclipses Certainty

I HAVE NOW completed all the paperwork for admission to the memory care facility and provided the necessary deposit.

Check.

Obtained the signatures of two physicians.

Check.

It is time—but it isn't.

Because along comes Covid-19.

By this time, in early March of 2020, the virus has already begun decimating nursing homes. Memory care facilities are no longer admitting residents as they try to figure out how to isolate patients who contract the virus in order to protect other residents and staff.

Alan is still at home. We are now in limbo. In the next period of waiting, my major issue is not just my fretting over the

Novel Coronavirus and the stay-at-home order our state decreed on March 19. Keeping an eye on my husband is now a full-time and sleepless job for me, 24-7. Even if Ryan, who is certified by his home care company during a time of Covid, still provides relief for me during three half-days a week, whenever he arrives, I crash and take naps.

Alan's condition worsens. We cannot drive to any destination that might engage his interest because simply taking a drive has its own delusional hazards. At home, he intensifies one of his "jobs," which is wrecking things around the house. He becomes obsessed with moving things around, grabbing armfuls of clothes from his or my closet and dropping them in heaps anywhere and everywhere. One day he stuffed an armload in the garbage can. When I pulled them out, they were sodden and rank.

I can only lock so much stuff in the guest room, with the open sofa bed where I now sleep, or in my small office, where I still have to manage bills and paperwork and schedules. The next time Ryan is covering for me, I load the trunk of the car with all but our most basic clothes, along with breakable and precious objects like my good china and make a run to the new storage space.

But these are replaceable. Just things, after all.

A few weeks after declaration of our state's stay-at-home order, the Los Angeles Press Club invites writers to submit essays about life in a time of Covid. I decide to participate—and not only participate, but I realize this is my chance to get the word out about life as a caregiver spouse, as well as about Lewy body dementia. It will be my first attempt at outreach, at advocacy. I culled notes from my journal. The result was an essay that appeared on the L.A. Press Club's website:

"His Crowd Flouts Social Distance"

Today Alan asked, for the umpteenth time, "Why can't we go to our restaurant?" meaning his favorite place, which happens to be shuttered.

"It's closed, because of the Novel Coronavirus."

"The what?"

"The pandemic. Coronavirus. Covid-19." I repeat all three, hoping one will click. "Most of the nation is staying home, you know."

But that's a slip-up on my part, because my husband does not know. During the past month, while we've been sheltering in place, he has further lost his grip on reality. My husband has dementia. I am his primary caregiver.

And we are far from alone. Alzheimer's afflicts an estimated 5.8 million Americans as of 2019, meaning that for many in this nation the incurable disease has overtaken a spouse, or a member of their close or extended family.

In our house, every day has become a Groundhog Day scenario of erase, repeat, erase. Inescapable news for the rest of us peels away from his memory. We subscribe to two print newspapers, and he pages through them but does not retain. Headlines do not sink in for this retired math professor and member of Mensa, nor do the top stories on nightly PBS news, though at dinnertime from habit he goes through the motions of watching.

There are several kinds of dementia, and all involve confusion and memory loss. *His affliction, however, is not the brand-name dementia of the better-known Alzheimer's but the second largest variant. Alan has Lewy body dementia (LBD), the incurable disease that afflicts 1.3 million Americans. One was actor Robin Williams. Undergoing the dreadful disease characteristics of confusion and paranoia led him to take his own life.*

Paranoia permeates our household. My husband asks daily, "Who are you?" and I say, "I am your wife of 23 years," to which he comes back with, "Not possible!" I bring out our marriage certificate, which he dismisses it as a forgery, "a swindle."

Another hallmark of LBD is hallucinations. While we stay home, practicing social distancing as a Census-count household of two, we daily host a not-so-fun party of uninvited guests. The house bustles with so-called 'phantom boarders,' and to him they are real. No point in trying to dissuade him.

According to him, they arrive for meals, steal things, turn drawers inside out, appear outside windows. Sometimes, he says, they threaten him. They are of all ages and genders, former co-workers and girlfriends, people young and old, and some are family members long since dead. Sometimes he calls them out by name.

His dementia began to appear around 2016, and as it progressed we gradually shucked activities in a list that sounds like restrictions from Covid-19. He stopped driving (not without a fight), and we gave up air travel. We stopped attending plays and concerts and movies for these became too complicated because of trips to the rest room and chances of getting lost in a crowd. We reduced our restaurant attendance to one place, his favorite, where the servers knew the situation, the place that is now shuttered.

Before March of this year, I didn't imagine that I was practicing for home-stay confinement, then the virus shackled us further — yet by a small degree. Since then we venture out for an occasional drive-thru lunch or a mid-afternoon Starbucks latte and petite vanilla bean scone.

But one thing hasn't changed. We still take short walks in our back yard, and I say short, because his gait is now affected by his illness. Once upon a time we were scuba divers, birders, hikers. Now, trails and parks closed? We couldn't manage those anyway, not now.

Yet silver linings can be found almost anywhere, if you dig for them. The bright spot in our home confinement, before and during Covid-19, has been the monarch butterfly garden we've maintained in our yard for the past half dozen years.

Lately, the milkweed is festooned with a dozen yellow and black striped caterpillars.

And if you look closely you'll see the surprise of little green chrysalises, like so many miniature celadon vases, dangling from branches, under window ledges, secured on a wooden trellis, attached by a short silken cord to the handle of a watering can or the edge of a brick. Within a week or so each one will emerge as an iconic orange, black and white monarch butterfly, offsetting the serious downside of our lives like some kind of miracle, a hopeful sign that in the larger scheme of things, life goes on.

Lives are in upheaval across the nation, but there is some comfort in knowing that in your particular circumstances you are not alone. Parents know there are countless moms and dads who find themselves suddenly home-schooling. Couples with mandated work-at-home tasks on laptops and desktops know they are vying for focus in the limited space of a residential address, as are many others. I, too, know I am not alone. I am just one of the family caregivers trying to keep a loved one with dementia safe.

These weeks of further restriction with scant relief seems to be hastening my husband's decline, though losing his grip on reality was inevitable. It might have taken longer, a reprieve for both him and our marriage thanks to a few more nights out at his favorite restaurant. A few more movies, where once seated he'd fall asleep. Still, we were together, a couple, almost like the good old days, before this home confinement hit, before they hit. I mean dementia. I mean Covid-19.

And now, when the phantom boarders start to crowd us, flouting the six-foot rule of social distance, I have begun saying, "Tell them to go away. They are breaking the rules. The rules of the pandemic, Covid-19, the virus."

Fugitive

It is now April 2020. He keeps trying to run away. If I try to stop him, his compulsion morphs into rage. It is like the moment when he thought his daughter and I were federal agents trying to haul him off to prison.

Now I face this level of confrontation any time, day or night, when my once tender and caring husband begins glaring at me, his eyes radiating hate. Even with the half-days of Ryan's help, I am emotionally and physically exhausted.

I lock the exterior doors of the house from the inside and keep the keys on my belt, which he tries to wrest away from me. But doors present no barrier because there are windows through which he tries to escape. Their design means that only if I have them covered from the outside with, say, plywood, might I prevent his going through. I am not yet ready to board up the house as if for Hurricane Al, the storm inside my walls.

Keeping him home and safe becomes a desperate game of whack-a-mole. I sit guard in the living room, keeping an eye on the bay window, the easiest one for him to use as an exit. When I need a bathroom break, that's when he'll try to seize the moment and climb through.

I'm not usually a praying person, but I pray for the memory care facilities in this state to find a way to admit new residents in a time of Covid. I offer up my plea of please, somebody, do something—but until that happens, I have to come up with my own solution for his safety and to save my sanity.

I devise one, but it only works in the daytime. I move the car to the front of the driveway and sit in it. From there I can see the house from a wide angle. If he escapes, he'll have to cross my line of vision. The car becomes a refuge, where I listen to music or phone a close friend and cry through my desperation while, at the same time, staying vigilant.

Often, he does get out, and if I don't notice this immediately, then a neighbor on either side or across the street—we are all on Covid stay-at-home orders and they are all aware of our situation—will text me. I'll hear a ping and get a text message: Al is outside again.

Despite his balance issues, he can make his way through the neighborhood like long-legged lightning. The saving grace again is GPS. When I help him dress in the mornings, I make sure he has his iPhone in his belt holster.

When he runs away, I drive around and eventually find him. Sometimes he will be talking—not with or to, but at—some bewildered homeowner warily standing on their porch and wondering about this semi-disheveled older man whose antic speech is articulate but makes no sense, and who, if asked, does not remember his home address.

One kindly woman offered to call his home. He handed her his iPhone, and she found the emergency asterisk with my number in Contacts and called me.

Usually, once I have found him and after a few minutes of curbside arguing, I can persuade him to join me in the car because I just happen to be on my way for a drive-thru Dunkin' Donut, or maybe Del Taco.

One day I am in the car tracking him down and looking at Find My Friend when I pull up by an address where the indicator says he should be standing. But no one is there. Then I notice that the Friend signal is inside the boundary of this large property dotted with orange trees. I recognize it as the home of the mayor of our city. The gate of a long, tree-lined driveway is open, and apparently Alan has ambled onto the grounds. What if my husband is mistaken for an intruder and the police are called? Does the mayor have armed security?

I phone Alan and by luck he remembers how to push the green button to answer.

"Honey," I say as calmly as I can, "I think you are on the mayor's property. I happen to be driving by, just outside. Why don't you come along with me and we'll get a latte and some vanilla scones at Starbucks?"

Welcome to another shoe-drop moment. Now I've learned that during one of his escape adventures he is likely to trespass. This time he comes willingly to the car, and we drive away and have a treat, and I don't berate him because it would do no good.

Once we are back home, he is tired and heads inside, while I resume my car-in-the driveway position and phone the city police. I inform them about my husband's dementia and how he has unwittingly walked onto private property. I say I am having difficulty keeping him from wandering, so it might happen again.

"He wears a Medic Alert on a chain around his neck," I tell the police. "It has his name and condition and my phone number, but someone might not bother to look, or he might take it off." This information is now on record, giving me a mild sense of relief.

Nighttime is the worst. Not being fully dressed, he doesn't have his iPhone on his belt, so no GPS. Plus, it is difficult to see him on residential streets in the dark. The first time he escapes after dark, I drive around and around until, luckily, I find him.

Clearly, I needed overnight help because I can't live without sleep. But it is nearly impossible to hire extra caregivers in a time of Covid. Ryan is able to add one more half-day, and every time he arrives for one of his shifts, I crash and sleep.

At night, I manage to stay awake on the living room sofa, sitting up under quilts, guarding the bay window, also keeping the nearest side window open a crack so I can listen for movement if he climbs out on that side of the house.

Then comes the night when Alan approaches me in my nest of quilts. It isn't him, this person steely eyed with fury, in a menacing stance. When I asked him to please stop, he keeps advancing until he is inches away from me. In that moment of dark epiphany, I fear for my life.

I am living in a war zone in need of male help at night, someone strong enough to stop Alan if he tries to escape or harm me. I need someone to protect me. I beg the home care service for emergency help, and—thank God—a male home caregiver becomes available, short-term only. I hire him. He is beefy and professional, and after their first encounter, Alan backs down.

When, oh, when, would the memory care facility finally figure out the Covid-isolation dilemma and start admitting new residents?

Then I get the call.

Placement Day

THE PHONE CALL came from Westwinds. I learned that a solution had been found for accepting new patients. For me, the message contained both good news and bad news.

The good news: this chain of memory care facilities would be dedicating an entire floor to new placements in one of their locations. These residents would remain in quarantine for two weeks to be sure they were Covid-free. I was assured that after the two-week quarantine, my husband would be transferred to the original location near our home, the one I wanted and for which I'd specifically signed a contract.

Then the bad news: I had carefully scripted a transition plan for one *specific* location, and I had already introduced Alan to that facility in an indirect and nonthreatening way. We had attended two pleasant receptions featuring music, wine, and hors d'oeuvres. If I mentioned having a nice lunch there with Ryan, I expected Alan to willingly walk through that same front door again. Or at least that was what I had envisioned: a carefully crafted transition plan almost guaranteed to work.

Trouble was, this *other* facility for the quarantine period was in a beach community thirty miles north of our home.

How could I get Alan to buy into it? How could I craft a loving lie that would account for this longish drive, then once we had arrived at the strange building, expect him to walk inside? Worse, I couldn't even walk him through the door, because the isolation building was under strict Covid-19 constraints. But I knew who might be able to walk inside with him. That was Ryan, whose service was certified as a caregiver for this same company. I asked him if it would be possible for him to help us at the other facility, and he said he would check with his supervisor. The best purely good news I had heard in a very long time came when he told me the answer was *Yes.*

Now I had to play my cancer card again, and I had one week to make a convincing new fictional case: I told Alan, repeatedly, that I was worried about my "follow-up surgery." That it would take place at a specialized clinic located thirty miles north.

I explained that during this "second surgery," because neither Cathy nor Ryan could help during my recovery, I had arranged for Alan to stay near my hospital. Ryan would accompany us for our check-ins. The C word held weight. My husband didn't object. This plan looked like the third greatest workaround of all.

May 14, 2020. Ryan will be here soon.

The day has arrived, a day I've dreaded ever since I first understood the cruel arc of my husband's affliction.

Early this morning, I packed an overnight bag for him, and one for me, too. He believes this stay is only for "a couple of nights."

As a distraction, I'm adding my iPad to his overnight kit. I've attached a few simple labels to help him navigate, though he won't manage unless a caregiver helps him. Still, it is a show of good faith, and I pretend he can open the TV app that will give him access to his obsessively favorite commentary show. Packing the iPad is a useful fiction.

Plus, at this moment, fiddling with the device is a distraction for me, a focus for my own distress. Today requires that I tell a terrible but necessary lie.

The drive begins, with me behind the wheel and Alan in the passenger seat next to me, with Ryan in the back seat. I want to touch my husband's hand, but I am navigating the freeway. After the first miles north on the I-405, the connection over a surface street is a long one, and for that I am glad. I have ample opportunity to touch his warm hand as we drive this last stretch before we reach our destination.

Now we are there. I pull into the semi-circular driveway by the entrance. I kiss Alan and simulate a casual tone with "See you soon." The two men get out near the main door of this multi-story building, and Alan begins walking at a slow and uneven pace.

Then it looks like I am driving away, supposedly toward a nearby clinic for my surgery, but instead I do a quick loop and pull into the parking area. From here, I can see Ryan and Alan as they walk toward the door, Ryan holding Alan's hand. Now my husband disappears inside, trusting as a lamb, spiking my guilt.

I wait in the parking lot. And wait. Our arrival had been planned for the distraction of lunchtime, and Ryan had cautioned me it might take at an hour or more to get Alan settled.

Finally, Ryan reappears, and I pull the car up to the entrance, where he climbs into the front passenger seat. "It went well," he says, before I even have a chance to ask. "They immediately offered him an ice cream and he lit up, then he saw the resident cat, a calico with a half-black mask. The cat walked right up to him like an old friend."

"Thank goodness."

"It gets better. He was so funny. Several staff members were on hand to greet him, and he turned to me and whispered, guy-to guy, 'Nice looking women here, don't you think?'"

I laugh, grateful like never before for comic relief. "What about his room? Did he cooperate with that part? Getting settled?"

"Turns out, his windows overlook the ocean. When he saw it, he said, 'What a magnificent view.' And the cat followed him into his room."

"No kidding." I could hardly believe it, or believe how my spirits rose.

"And the facility has a secure balcony with a telescope," Ryan adds. "He loved that."

I'm thinking: Better than I could have hoped or planned.

Yet as we drive southward on that long, connecting surface street before getting back on the I-405, it hits me hard: *my husband will never come home again.* I start crying, and when I see a safe place, I pull to the side of the road. Ryan, empathetic as always, comforts me. He offers tissues.

We arrive home, and I park at the front of the driveway. Then Ryan and I say our goodbyes. When he gets in his car and I watch him drive away, I am hit with another wave of loss because I am losing him too.

Before I pull into the garage, I notice something on the driveway, a fat yellow-and-black caterpillar. It is trundling along, trying to cross the concrete but veering toward a dangerous spider-ridden bush. I get out and do one of our interventions, lifting the caterpillar and carrying it to a safe spot.

This helps me get centered. I tell myself that Alan, like the caterpillar, is in a safe place, though it took an intervention to ensure his safety and mine, though he had to be spirited away from our home and left behind with a lie.

I am told I cannot call or email or text Alan—no patient phones are allowed at the facility, and it is way too soon for me to contact him, anyway. But I can text Ryan. The next day, May 15, I take a photo and send it to Ryan with this message:

> A beautiful new butterfly today! Thank you again, Ryan, for being so wonderful to Alan and such a great help to me. I don't know what I would have done without you.

> He replies, *Forever happy to have been part of our little team.*

Chapter 10
METAMORPHOSIS

I Heard About This at My Support Group

MY SUPPORT GROUP had begun to meet remotely on Zoom in April. By mid-May, my husband was in a memory care facility, and I was no longer caring for him at home. This did not mean the end of questions, however. Far from it, though my concerns and need for knowledge took a different turn.

One such concern was a rare but alarming change in Alan's behavior that would surface within a few weeks. By then I had heard similar stories shared by other members of the support group, so I was better prepared when it happened.

Events led up to this. After he had spent two weeks of mandatory Covid isolation in the high-rise clinic setting—with his "magnificent view" of the Pacific, the butterscotch kitty sleeping nightly on his bed, and the telescope on the secured balcony to engage his attention—my husband's next trip would be a van ride thirty miles south to the original memory care location near our home. The van ride, I was told, went smoothly.

Once he was settled in, I thought, we might adapt to a kind of life despite physical separation. This memory care residence has a far different ambiance from that of the quarantine facility, which was adjacent to a hospital complex. This is a single-story residence, and even in a time of Covid, I was told, family members would be permitted to visit loved ones for a "patio visit" while observing the required social distance. I envisioned the scene, with me sitting on a chair on one side of the wrought iron patio fence, and on the other side my husband, his balance ensured by a caregiver standing by. Or that was my plan.

Then, too, this was the same place I had selected after comparing facilities on my fake-article-research tour. I liked its policy of keeping friendly animals on the premises, and there was also the importance of location, less than a ten-minute drive from our home. It had an Old California charm, with both outside and center courtyards so residents could take walks yet remain secure. I had requested a room with a sliding door that opened onto the center courtyard.

When I decided on this company and this particular location—over a year ago, which felt like a minute wrapped up inside an eon—I had envisioned visiting Alan every day. Before the pandemic hit, I had also imagined joining him for an occasional lunch or dinner, maybe taking him for a short stroll in the nearby, charming Old Town area, maybe walking among the blooms at the nearby plant nursery where we'd always bought milkweed for our butterfly garden. Picturing us together this way had kept me moving forward, scenes of pleasant activities playing on the screen of my mind.

For months, I'd held onto such magical thinking, always assuming he would be compliant and willing and cooperative, never imagining that he would deny knowing me, much less see me as a stranger out to do him harm. Now, with Covid constraints, I'd need to wait for a visit with the patio fence between us, at least until he became oriented to his new home. And so, I was told, I should be patient and let him settle in.

Counting his time in quarantine, three weeks had passed, and I was eager to see him, eager for him to see me, though I was both anxious and worried. His recent rejection of me made contacting him and his possible reaction a problem.

I was primed for our first visit, ready to reinforce my cover story about how my "second surgery" had gone well, if he even asked about it, and if he did ask or remember, then I would segue into a comment like "Now it is *your* turn for treatment."

With both hope and apprehension, therefore, I waited for the go-ahead from the facility's family coordinator, waited to make my first contact with my husband. At first, according to the daily reports, Alan was on the way to adjustment. His room had been decorated with care in the hope that the special photographs and objects I had brought over would resonate with him in a comforting way.

For the Memory Box—a glass-front display box positioned outside the door of every resident's room—I'd selected family photographs: the two of us in happier times and some photos of his daughter with her husband and the two grandchildren. There were also a few tactile items in the box. One was his precious miniature of Wrigley Field, the baseball stadium near where he had grown up. As a kid, he'd snuck into games in such late innings that no one shooed him away.

I'd also chosen framed prints and photographs for the walls of his room. One photo was from his skydiving days, another of his daughter on a roller coaster. Another piece was a plein air painting of Catalina Island, one of several we had purchased during weekends we'd enjoyed on the island.

I was assured daily that he was settling in.

Then I started hearing a different kind of report: he was having trouble sleeping. More than merely trouble sleeping. He was up at night, sometimes all night. Wandering the halls. Also poking into other residents' rooms, both by day and by night. This was not good. He was not settling in. Worse, he was starting to show bursts of aggression.

This is where advice from the support group comes in. I was aware of the direction, in unusual cases, that Alan's behavior might lead. I knew from the reports of others in my group and from our leader Audrey that this kind of behavior might trigger admission to a "geripsych unit," which is to say, the geriatric psychiatry section of a hospital, where meds and behavior could be monitored and adjusted. I hoped it wouldn't come to this, but if it did, then at least I was prepared and would not be blindsided.

For now, I was told by the memory care facility, Alan would need to be monitored more closely to stop him from wandering at night and bothering the other residents. I was also advised that he needed additional nighttime coverage. Taking a big gulp, I agreed to hundreds of dollars in extra night shifts, and because this was on top of a five-figure monthly residency fee, at first I wondered if this was just an additional source of revenue for Westwinds. Remembering Alan's menacing stance at home, I added the private care, still thinking this would be temporary. Just until he settled in.

As luck would have it, one of the private caregivers during this time of crisis turned out to be none other than our friend Ryan. The first day he was assigned to my husband, Ryan said Alan had recognized him right away. He sent me a text with an attached selfie shot and, by pure coincidence, both were wearing shirts printed with little dinosaurs. We had purchased Alan's shirt at the Natural History Museum years ago.

Even though the image of the two of them, arm in arm, brought tears to my eyes, I told myself this sartorial coincidence was a good sign. I had not been able to reach out in any way to my husband since the day he entered Westwinds. Yet now with Ryan as my liaison, I thought maybe, maybe, I could finally connect with Alan, at least on FaceTime. I was still a bit wary, though, because I knew Alan became confused and did not respond well to any kind of teleconferencing, whether telemedicine or a family call on Zoom. Still, it was worth a try.

Ryan knew how desperate I was to make contact. He recognized my separation anxiety layered on top of guilt. When we got an okay from the facility director, we planned the FaceTime chat for June 9. Ryan would make the call to me, holding his iPhone and monitoring the conversation in case it went sideways. I prepared a kind of conversational script. When that much-anticipated day came, Ryan texted me that morning: *We'll have to cancel the FaceTime call. He is having trouble today.*

The nature of that trouble was Alan's aggression, and it was getting worse. This was my former lifeguard, my tender-hearted husband. And yet not long ago he had threatened me with an iron rod. As his aggression escalated, I was updated throughout the day.

That night, Alan was transported by ambulance to a geriatric psychiatric hospital for an intensive two-to-three-week course of treatment.

I couldn't see him while he was in treatment because of Covid constraints. I couldn't see him via FaceTime because of his disorientation. If I phoned, he didn't know me. It was the worst three weeks since the beginning of May. I feared that I would never again catch even a momentary glimpse of my husband, of the man he had been. How could I remember his greatness?

After Alan's hospital stay in the geripsych unit, I was told that because of Covid rules he would require another two-week quarantine before he could return to the memory care community near our home. Now my head was spinning from all this relocation business, and I couldn't imagine how disorienting it must have been for him, or if he were even aware.

But this time the quarantine came with a concealed gift.

A few months ago, Westwinds had opened a new facility not far from our home. It was sunny and, being new, still underpopulated. It had a residential floor and a separate floor for quarantined residents. This is where Alan was taken following his hospital stay.

When the required two weeks had passed, he was cleared to join other residents in the memory care community. This cheerful and spacious new location appeared to be the best of all possible placements for him. Rather than relocating him again, I arranged for him to stay there. In a way, and by accident, and even thanks to the harsh rules of Covid, we'd found the clean, well-lighted place I had hoped someday to find for my husband.

A Change of Season

AFTER THE INITIAL spring abundance of caterpillars in all sizes clinging to the leaves of our milkweed plants, and often spotted by sharp-eyed Ryan during his care giving days here, Alan's absence coincided with a lull in the appearance of the monarchs. Two important parts of my world seemed to shrink all at once.

I was living alone in the house now, mainly staying inside. Outdoors, I could find few caterpillars, and no chrysalises with their celadon and gold promise of a beautiful emergence. Occasionally, a male monarch butterfly visited a bloom for nectar, then flitted on. But if there were eggs, I didn't see them hatch. I couldn't find any of the stripy little yellow-and-black caterpillars that I loved to observe and watch over.

As the months of the pandemic wore on, the reason for this dearth of monarchs became more apparent. The milkweed was being passed over because it was unwelcoming, because it had been neglected. Alan had labored at controlling nasty bugs, but now there were masses of aphids and clusters of the larvae of the awful red and black bugs. Big insects I hadn't noticed before had also moved in. Katydids and grasshoppers and walking sticks, carnivores that gobble caterpillar eggs and little monarch larvae. It seemed as if the female monarchs were skipping over this deteriorated milkweed patch with good cause. It was getting late in the season to start new plants and would be a daunting task to restore the butterfly garden. Besides, I was depressed and despondent most days and didn't feel up to the task.

Instead, because our garden no longer offered consolation, I looked for other kinds of respite through nature. After checking online to be sure my plan was okay under Covid rules, I decided I would start walking outdoors in a place that most resembled wilderness but was only a twenty-minute drive away. This was a site Alan and I had visited many times for birding and guided nature walks, the San Joaquin Marsh in Irvine, with its half-dozen large settling ponds that attract local and migrating waterfowl. It also has a large butterfly garden with native plants where I could see a riot of monarchs and other beauties and just stand and admire them or preserve them through the lens of my camera.

Walking the trails alone, as I began doing early on Monday mornings that spring, became a healing routine that helped lift me out of depression. Walking solo along the miles of trails, I rarely saw another human being, at most maybe two in an hour, and they were usually alone, too, with binoculars dangling around their necks and maybe toting a long-lens camera. Monday mornings became the predictable event that took the place of seeing Alan when the memory care facilities did not yet allow visits because of the pandemic.

Instead, I visited the giant egret and watched him drying his wings, spread open in the sun. I watched the green heron while he stalked little fish, waiting like a statue on a log protruding from the pond. Sometimes I caught a glimpse of the resident family of osprey in their huge platform nest. One day I walked farther than usual, all the way to the other side of the sanctuary. The scene opened out onto the pond with its pelican island, behind which no buildings were tall enough to reveal that this landscape was in the city. The photograph I took looked like I had taken the shot in open country, hundreds of miles away from civilization.

Meanwhile, back in our own butterfly garden, the infestations continued and the remaining milkweed deteriorated. I began ripping out the exhausted plants, and as they came out, I prepared the soil for the future.

The long-anticipated day finally arrived when the facility received approval from the county health department to schedule family visits. For the first time in three months, I would be allowed to see my husband in person.

I was scheduled for a half-hour visit on Thursday, August 11, with me on one side of a decorative wrought iron fence. On the other side, Alan would sit in the patio at a Covid-safe distance, accompanied by a caregiver. I would wear a mask. This appointment, now posted in my calendar, lifted some of my crushing sense of guilt for what seemed like neglecting him, although with the pandemic I'd had no choice. Despite my mask, Alan would see my eyes and hear my voice. I hoped he would maybe feel less abandoned. But did he ever feel abandoned? I'd heard no such report. During the past twelve weeks, whenever I'd asked, I'd been told, "No, he hasn't asked for you yet." The reply both hurt and consoled me, because if he didn't miss me, then that was a relief ... but if he didn't miss me, then he'd forgotten me. That is the paradox of being the wife of a patient with advanced dementia.

Before my date to see Alan in person, as it turned out, his daughter Cathy would be my trailblazer. On the Sunday before my appointment, she was scheduled for an afternoon Zoom meeting with her dad despite his antipathy for Zoom contact. Two senior Westwinds team would be with Alan to make the call.

Cathy would appear live on a computer screen from two thousand miles away. No social distance needed, no need for her to wear a mask, so I was hopeful that her familiar face and voice would awaken a spark of recognition when she said, "Hi, Dad. It's me, Cathy!"

I imagined him responding with his familiar, "Hello, Sweets!" I hoped for an echo of that recognition when, four days later at my first appointment, I would say, "Hi, Honey. It's me, Allene!" Maybe I would also hear, "Hello, Sweets," his affectionate greeting for both of us. That was as far as my hopes extended that week.

Cathy's Zoom visit ... well, let's just say it did not go as hoped. She was able to see her dad, and after three months, that gave her some comfort. But he closed his eyes, visually shutting her out, showing no sign of recognition. After a few minutes, he said, "I like your voice. I think you have a European accent." Of course, she has no such an accent, and his words seemed disappointingly meager, but she carried on, talking about her garden, her work as a school librarian, the grandchildren. She was prepared for him to ask about them as babies, though both were now in college, but on his end of the call they were never mentioned. She chatted on alone to fill the conversational void.

I was prepared for a similar disappointment the following Thursday, when I'd have a half-hour in-person meeting. Alan might not know me as his wife, but I wanted him to want to be with me, even if we were separated by a fence. Ever since my Alzheimer's support group had suggested it, I'd even imagined anonymously flirting with my once-flirty husband.

It would be hot in the afternoon at 1 p.m., my appointed time, so I strategically chose a summery outfit. A blouse with a V-neck in the flattering color of cerise. My best-fitting jeans. A pair of straw espadrilles with jaunty high heels that I rarely wear. But if I wanted to flirt with my husband, I figured now was the time. For luck, I added the necklace Cathy had given me for my birthday.

When I arrived, I called the office to let them know I had pulled into the staff parking lot. I was instructed to drive around to the other side and park close to the patio, where I saw to my surprise that the spaces on that end were empty. *Of course,* I thought, *because I am the only permitted visitor right now.* If not for a time of Covid, the visitor parking spaces would be full, and family members would be inside visiting their loved ones.

Staff were there to greet me. For this day's visitors, they had set up two pretty, canopy-bedecked welcome tables, both with bouquets of fresh flowers. One table held water, masks, and a sign-in-sheet with the usual medical questions requiring answers and a signature. The other table held petite sandwiches and pastries suitable for a substantial tea service—along with the sandwiches, tiny sweet and savory tarts, mini-crab cakes, chocolate in several variations, plus other delicacies displayed to please the eye.

"These are so beautiful," I said, though I was too nervous with anticipation to eat any of them. Still, it set the scene for a celebratory mood, and that was the point. The arriving families always needed bucking up. Many of us had not seen our loved ones since the Covid shutdown months ago.

Near the welcome tables, the staff had created a collage on the exterior of a plate glass window. It consisted of candid photos of individual residents taken in moments of laughter or caught with smiles that suggested something like contentment. Each picture was mounted on a scalloped paper backing like a colorful, wiggly frame. It reminded me of something I couldn't quite place, but it formed a cheerful collage that filled the large window. I walked closer. There was Alan's photograph, looking happy. I felt hopeful.

"We also have a little gift for you after you see Alan," said one of the senior staff. "His caregiver will escort him to the patio any minute."

As if on cue, a glass door opened and out came a charming young woman named Katie, a senior staff member who sometimes doubled as an escort for visits. She turned and held the door open, and Alan stepped onto the patio. I had received recent photographs of him by text, so I wasn't entirely surprised to see that he had become more visibly frail. It didn't seem possible that just over a year ago, he had still been capable of doing his hour-long, twice-weekly laps in the health club's swimming pool.

I also noticed that his walk had become more unsteady than I remembered. Katie hovered close while he positioned himself in the chair. He had trouble with balance, and it looked like he was feeling his way rather than looking to see where he was going. She patted him on the shoulder to guide and reassure him. Then she nodded at me to begin the visit.

"Hi, Alan, honey," I said. "It's me. Allene."

He didn't look toward me or react in any way. Instead, he repositioned himself in the chair and closed his eyes.

"Would you like a glass of water?" Katie asked him. When he nodded, she poured from a nearby pitcher and handed him the plastic glass. He took a sip. He held it in his mouth, noisily swished it around, then spat it out forcefully in my direction. It landed like a tiny cloudburst on the patio between us.

I recoiled in surprise and alarm. Was this a physical rejection of me? Last April, he had called me an impostor, a swindler, so was my very presence here reawakening this false perception? "What he just did," my voice squeaked, "what does that mean?"

Katie replied, "I'd say it means nothing, really."

Then he did it again, and once more after that, draining the plastic cup. *The gesture might have meant nothing to her, but it wasn't nothing to me.*

After he ran out of water, I chattered about random matters to this shell of my husband. I directed a couple of pre-planned questions to him, but when these didn't elicit a response, I tried short riffs from my list. One was about gardening, how I was growing big red tomatoes.

"Tomatoes," he said, his eyes still squeezed shut.

That was something! Maybe one word was all I would hear this time. If so, then I'd take his word and remember it when I tended my tomatoes, probably when I cultivated tomatoes for a long time to come.

In addition to this minimal exchange, there was a curious moment when Alan tapped into his old, verbal precision. I asked about the bird, one of three resident pets, along with a little terrier named Jelly and a long-haired bunny named Chewy. I'd seen a texted photograph showing Alan with the bird perched on his hand, and the caption in the text read, *Alan and Buddy the parakeet.*

So I asked, "Do you like Buddy the parakeet?"

At my question, his head snapped toward Katie and he said to her, professorially, "*Not* a parakeet."

"No, you're right, Alan," Katie said, then she looked toward me. "We had the species wrong. We found out Buddy's a cockatoo."

After that surprising moment of commentary, Alan suddenly fell asleep and couldn't be roused. I said, "Goodbye, Alan, I love you," to the sleeping figure slumped in the chair, but I doubt he heard me. My half hour was over. A white Styrofoam box had appeared on the tea table. "Please, take all you want," Katie said, so I half-filled the take-away box for my dinner, thinking about the tradition of feeding people after a funeral, at a wake, and providing food to comfort the grieving souls. I didn't know how I could be hungry, but I was.

Then another staff member appeared and handed me the aforementioned gift, a heavy square box of the type that holds a whole take-home pie. "It's apple," she said. "Our culinary director is great with pastries." By coincidence, apple was Alan's favorite, and another remorseful thought struck me: I could enjoy this, but if he ate a serving of pie now, it would not be in the form of a flaky crust and tender chunks of cinnamon apples. It would have to be served pureed.

I'd been told earlier that week that my husband had experienced two choking incidents, one of which had required the Heimlich maneuver. A specialist had come in to consult, and Alan was now on a special pureed diet to avoid choking risk.

Taped to the box containing what felt like my selfish pie were two photographs, one showing Alan looking amused, the other seeming contented. Both were mounted on colorful scalloped paper, like the photos displayed on the window. Now I remembered what these colorful paper frames reminded me of: crafts in elementary school, projects thumb-tacked on a bulletin board. Maybe this was fitting, because most residents at this memory care facility would eventually become like little children.

I took the long way home via surface streets rather than getting on the freeway because I knew I might cry, and when I did, I pulled to the curb under a tree.

The longer drive also gave me time to reflect on the visit, and after returning home, I called Cathy and gave her a report ... of how he had said even fewer words to me than to her. Twelve words to her, one word to me, or call it three, counting the correction of bird species, which Cathy and I both found endearing. It was so like the Alan we knew, to be precise in terminology.

But mainly, what his daughter and I had in common was that he did not know us. "He had his eyes closed the entire time," I said. "As he did during the Zoom session with you."

Now Cathy and I began to hatch a plan for next time, a plan for each of us. Because her call and my visit were both in the afternoon, we decided his eyes-closed condition might be about the time of day, naptime after lunch, so we would request morning appointments.

She didn't wear a mask on Zoom, but I did in person, so I would request permission to wear a mask with a clear insert.

The facility director gave me a morning appointment. Because so many families had to be accommodated, mine would take place in two weeks' time. She approved the clear mask insert, and also approved my idea of playing music as a way I hoped to connect with Alan, though I hadn't yet worked out how I would accomplish this.

The following week, I collected my kit with the half-clear mask and a small external speaker to amplify the music I wanted to play. I was almost ready for the following Thursday morning. It wasn't like I expected Alan to become his old self. I knew better. This was a progressive disease.

There sat my kit on a table by the door. And then came another milestone phone call.

It was the physician from the facility. "Don't be alarmed," he said. "Your husband is okay. I saw him again today. I just wanted to give you a call."

"Thank you," I said, appreciating how he stayed in touch. Then I heard the question that threw me.

"What is your overall goal of care?" the doctor asked.

"What do you mean?" I thought this might be about the pureed food, and it was, in a way.

"He is sleeping more, and for longer periods of time," said the doctor. "I think it is time to talk about hospice."

I was stunned. The word rang with such finality. In my mind, hospice equals death. But the doctor explained that it didn't mean Alan's passing was imminent. It has to do with adding services to keep him comfortable. He concluded our conversation by saying that my husband could be with us still for many months to come.

The Last Musicale

Remember their greatness. The support group adage has many meanings for me, and one is Alan's larger-than-life personality, his affinity for outsized pursuits.

As a boy growing up in Chicago with a single mother and scant means, for Alan there was nothing left over for culture or frills. Then a door opened into the world of opera, a sphere of spectacle and soul stirring music.

One day when he was a senior at all-boys Lane Tech High School and focused on math and science, he saw an announcement on a hallway bulletin board. It offered spot work for a few tall and athletic young men as spear-carriers, or supernumeraries, in a production by the Lyric Opera of Chicago. He swiftly applied and, being fit from competitive swimming and standing six-foot-three, he got the gig. As the announcement made clear, these were not speaking parts. He would be an extra, standing in the background.

I'm sure that the first time he walked onto the stage, costumed as a warrior for a dress rehearsal, he was not only swept into the imaginary universe of Giacomo Puccini but also transported out of his own limited life. On stage, the surfaces of tiaras and armor sparkled with reflected light as the principal cast members, clad in opulent fabrics, commanded the stage like demigods. The diva with her gem-threaded coif, swirling gown, and kohl-lined eyes, must have tugged at a young Alan's heart.

Come opening night, and there he was, a bit player in a performance that aroused the passion of hundreds of people wearing silken gowns and tuxedos, an audience that rose to their feet at the end of the opera with booming applause and cries of *bravo* and *brava* in a wave of love and approval. And he was a part of it all.

But the people and costumes paled next to the music. The arias. The arias. Longing and loss distilled into sound. They pierced him, poured into his bloodstream. The music would become a part of Alan for the rest of his life.

And there was another moment in this story that Alan liked to tell. He might not agree if we could debate it today, but I see this as a moment contributing to his out-of-the-box tendency to bend the rules. It had been made plain to him and the other young spear-carriers that although they had no speaking roles, they would be trained to brandish their weapons on cue. During the final dress rehearsal, the celebrated tenor Jussi Bjorling came up with his own improvised blocking. To execute a faux parry of sword and spear, he singled out Alan, to whom Bjorling said in mid-rehearsal, "Yell back!" It wasn't a speaking part, exactly, but from then until the closing performance, yelling back is what Alan did. And I think I saw an afterglow even decades later, as if a facet of his personality originated when he was granted permission to bend the rules by an operatic demigod.

Recently, when I was collecting photographs to scan for an online memorial of his life I was planning, I came upon a photo of Alan in his tux. It looked like he was born to wear one. He and I had been dating since we'd met in June of 1992, and by now it was autumn. As he was a long-time subscriber to Pacific Opera, his subscription included opening night with a gala dinner beforehand. The first opening night in our relationship was coming up.

"I'd love to go," I had said, knowing how important opera was to him. I'd heard the story of his spear-carrier initiation on our second date. For my part, I had long-ago attended performances of maybe three operas: Bizet's *Carmen* in Los Angeles, Mozart's *The Magic Flute* during a college trip to Europe, and I had endured Mussorgsky's *Boris Godounov* at the Met when I lived in New York. But that was it. Alan, however, had seen several of the major works more than once.

Sure, I thought, *I'd be glad to dress up in fancy black and come along for the ride*, even if— though I didn't say any of this out loud —I have never been much of an opera fan.

Over the next several years, season after season, immersion in the outsized operatic world grew on me. My breath caught as the curtain revealed the enormous sets. I abided the slow unrolling of the story while waiting for the thrill of a heart-stopping aria. I put together a pair of dressy black outfits, including a short jacket with opalescent black beads that caught the light. I embraced the whole experience each time, especially as I observed Alan's delight, as reliable as if opera bestowed on him a kind of unconditional love.

At the pre-performance fundraising dinners, I enjoyed meeting and conversing with interesting people. I also enjoyed glancing around the lobby during intermission to check out how other women were clad, and I appreciated seeing so many men turned out in formal wear, including my own date and later husband. But we all know that most guys look good in a tux.

Fast forward to how opera came back into my husband's life. Back when Alan had begun to slip, I had tried to glean as much knowledge as I could from reading and my support groups, and even from attending a couple of receptions to get an inside sense of memory care facilities. I've mentioned how one of those events featured musical entertainment where wine and hors d'oeuvres were served to the audience of two dozen or so, half of them visiting family members.

Alan, who would not become a resident at Westwinds until many months later, wondered why we were in attendance that day. I gave him my usual "I'm writing an article about assisted living for seniors." Again, he accepted my cover story. It helped that the singer booked for the reception was charming and skilled in delivering familiar Golden Oldies, accompanied by his backup tech ensemble. Yet the real star of the show turned out to be one of the impaired residents.

When Alan and I first arrived and found seats near the hors d'oeuvres table, this woman was seated on the other side of the room, somnolent and slumped in a wheelchair.

I scanned the room, smiling at other visiting family members. Whenever I glanced in that woman's direction, it seemed clear that she was in a very advanced state of dementia. No matter how her caregiver or her visiting husband coaxed her, this woman was nonverbal, out of it, somewhere else entirely. Gone. Once I saw her open her mouth and from across the room I heard a garbled sound.

Then the professional singer started his Golden Oldies show.

It is well established that music resides somewhere deep in the mind, tucked away in long-term memory. Among stutterers, even those with seriously impaired speech, some are known to sing smoothly and with perfectly recalled lyrics, even if they have trouble uttering a common sentence. This is also true for some dementia patients. On the day of that reception when the singer began his act with the 1950s chart-topper "Lipstick on Your Collar," I watched in amazement as the woman in the wheelchair suddenly sat up. She opened her eyes and began to sing, and not only was every word straight from that pop-chart song, but she carried it off robustly and in excellent pitch. What's more, she stood up, and with her husband and caregiver careful to keep her from going wild, she began to dance in front of her wheelchair. Alan and I and everyone else in the room cheered her on.

That took place early in 2019. So much has happened since then, and now it is 2020, and my husband is a resident in a similar facility but in a different location.

After my disappointment at the first patio visit, when he spewed water in my direction and closed his eyes, I was determined to make a difference at my next visit. I would bring music to play for him, and I would also bring a miniature speaker to amplify music from my iPhone. But what kind of music should that be?

I remembered the memory care resident with her Golden Oldies, belting out the lyrics and melody, but I had no reason to associate old pop songs with Alan. He listened to classical music. Okay, I had the streaming Bach station on my Pandora app, the soundtrack for my caregiver getaway days in my car, so at first I thought, well, maybe I'll play him a Bach cantata.

Then it struck me: A stirring voice. An aria.

And so it came to pass that on the day of my second visit, I came with opera in hand—this time in the morning when Alan was more alert. Maybe so, but his eyes still darted from side to side, not recognizing me, nor registering that someone he knew was standing in front of him barely six feet away, on the other side of the patio fence.

He suddenly launched into a confused and fragmented lecture as if he were speaking to a lecture hall suspended in the air. He chattered on about unrelated topics, his thoughts couched in articulate, fragmented phrases like shattered glass, shiny but broken.

Then I asked him, "Would you like to hear some music? I brought some along."

"Okay."

A response! At least this was a start, and when he didn't resume his fractured lecture, I considered this a favorable sign. I hastily navigated through an app on my iPhone, then opened it up: Pavarotti's voice beamed forth in the soaring aria "Nessun dorma" from Puccini's opera *Turandot*.

Alan took a deep breath. He was suddenly sitting still at a kind of silent attention. While he was enveloped, embraced, by one of the most beautiful arias in the world of opera, he turned to face me, his eyes calm and focused. We made eye contact and it held and I almost wept with relief and joy as the music played on. I played it over and over.

Afterward, when his caregiver asked, "Did you like the music?" Alan said, "Yes." Then he said, *"Die Walkure?"* I couldn't believe it. Was he making a request?

If so, he was referring to a different opera, one of Richard Wagner's four-opera, Ring Cycle, and I was pretty sure he meant "The Flight of the Valkyries." He and I had seen the entire cycle performed in successive evenings, an exhilarating yet, to me, exhausting cultural experience. That had been over a decade ago, but clearly the music was deeply embedded in his memory.

"Die Walkure?" I replied. "Yes. I'll bring music from that opera next time."

I glanced at my watch and saw that I still had a couple of minutes remaining in our half-hour visit. I restarted the "Nessun dorma" aria. Alan smiled. It felt to me as though he had moved into another room in his mind, a place where there might be space for me. It felt as if we were sitting together in the audience, him in his tux and me in my sparkly black beaded jacket, holding hands. I wanted to reach out and touch him but Covid rules didn't allow.

The aria ended and he was still looking directly at me. He knew *someone like me* was there. I took a chance. "I love you."

"Love you," he replied.

It didn't matter that he might have just been parroting my words, that he didn't know who I was, the person he'd just said he loved, or whether he had a glimmer of what those words even meant. He had made eye contact, and there was a feeling in the air between us, a space created by music. He had enabled me to speak and project my own words. That was plenty, plentiful, for a grateful me.

And that's how I found my way back to him the first time. Through music.

Then there was another surprise, a different kind of deep-seated connection.

Back on our second date, when Alan had invited me to see his house—it was a summer night in 1992—I was struck by the travel aspirations of this man. We entered through the back door, and once inside I couldn't miss the world map affixed to a large bulletin board. It filled one entire wall of his roomy service porch.

I must have stared. "The blue push pins are where I have been," he said, "and the green ones are where I intend to go."

That night I was driving my own car because we lived in adjacent cities about fifteen miles apart. After dining in a seaside restaurant is when he'd invited me to see his house, of which he was justly proud. I'd heard about his many modifications, like adding French doors in two rooms and a cozy window seat in the living room and planting several varieties of fruit trees. In the lingering mid-summer twilight, he said, I might still see them, or perhaps their silhouettes. He understood that I couldn't stay long and had to return home because I had an early meeting the next morning.

After a brief tour, which included the impossible-to-miss National Geographic world map, he said, "Before you leave here tonight, I want to show you something." He walked down the hall as I wondered what he'd gone to retrieve. Surely not the proverbial etchings because I thought there was nothing artsy about this guy, unlike many of my other friends.

No, it was his Scuba equipment, and high-quality gear at that. On our first date, we had established that both of us were cer-tified as sport divers, except he had notched about fifty entries in his logbook, far fewer for me. His dives had taken place in Hawaii and Mexico, mine, a few years back in the Florida Keys.

When I asked if some of the green pushpins on his map were future underwater sites, my question prompted a partial list. "Hope so," he said. "I'd like to dive Belize, Cozumel, Rangiroa—that's an atoll near Tahiti. And the Galapagos Islands."

That night, the metal on his regulator caught the living room light, and his array of gear—the plump-when-inflated buoyancy control device, the long fins—reminded me of a PBS nature show, with a bowerbird proffering bright objects to a prospective mate. The thought made me smile.

"Something funny?" he asked, seeming more curious than taken aback.

"It's just that your dive equipment is so ... so high quality. Mine is, well, I'd call it basic."

"Engineers like good gadgets," he said.

This display, I'll admit, promised future adventures together, so maybe the bowerbird effect worked. Within a few months, starting in Hawaii, we would begin a shared odyssey almost every year, whether on land or sea, that eventually encompassed two dozen countries.

Travel had been one of the most enduring and endearing themes of our marriage. I didn't know it yet, but a thread of that remained even as he lived apart from me at Westwinds.

During my first visit, he had closed his eyes and gone to his own far-away land. During the next two visits, I'd managed to lure him into a shared place when I cued up operatic arias. His eyes snapped open and he became alert, as if perhaps we were attending a performance at an opera house in Vienna or Barcelona, as we had during our travels. I don't know how the music worked its magic, but it tapped into something deep inside him, and I'd receive the gift of eye contact, a glimpse of a connection that lasted for a few precious words.

Then by accident rather than design, I found another sound cue that also drew him out, that summoned him from the depths of his cave.

That day at the memory care facility, I arrived at the scheduled time and took my customary chair facing the patio. Soon he appeared in the doorway with a caregiver holding his hand and escorting him out of the building and toward me. They sat on one side of the decorative wrought-iron fence, and I sat on the other side, looking in. When I said, "Hi, Alan, it's me, Allene," he gave no sign of recognition.

The residents wore personal clothing provided by their families, and when I noticed what he was wearing, it gave me an idea. The fabric had a repeating print of sea life, the kind we had seen through our masks during diving adventures off the coast of Ecuador, which was where we'd bought the shirt.

"Hammerhead sharks," I blurted out, "like the pattern on your shirt!" I said this with gusto, hoping it might get through to him. "We dove with hammerhead sharks in the Galapagos Islands." I was tempted to add the R word, *remember,* but we are told not to say this to dementia patients. Turns out I didn't need to.

Alan opened his eyes and said, "Galapagos" and "Hammerhead." I felt like I'd won the lottery again, and maybe I was on a roll, so I kept going, trying to hold his attention. "That was so much fun!"—fun being an upbeat, exclamation-worthy word but, truth was, that particular dive experience had involved too many sharks for my taste.

For his sake, but mainly for mine, I said it again: "Galapagos Islands. Hammerhead sharks!" and he repeated, "Galapagos. Hammerheads."

He was alert now. He didn't know who I was, but I had tapped into a vein of attention. I seized the moment again. "I love you," I said, and once again he parroted back, "Love you." Those two words made my day, made my week, would tide me over until I had a chance to see him again.

Returning from the memory care facility, I again avoided the freeway and took surface streets, where my reflexes could better manage reverie at 30 mph rather than 70. While traveling the five miles home, I felt as if the travel theme was pulling along other associations. Two thoughts popped into my head. One, recalling my bookselling days, was the title of a children's book by Dr. Seuss titled *Oh, the Places You'll Go*. The other was a musical phrase from the Frank Sinatra classic, "Come Fly With Me."

As I drove and hummed and bumbled along with the lyrics ("... up there ... we'll just glide"), I felt as excited as if I were planning our next trip. For the past quarter century, Alan and I had asked each other so many times, "Where should we go next?" In those years, some pushpin was always primed to turn from green to blue. The answer awaited us on the bulletin board with the sprawling National Geographic world map.

In Alan's world of Lewy body dementia, his tour guides now were his caregivers, his adventures limited to the rooms and hallways of a memory care facility. He would never be free to travel again. Still, on my future visits, I thought, *I'll invite him to join me on a magical tour of two-word snapshots.* Maybe he'd reply by repeating them back to me in a memory duet.

I began to wonder each time how many places we still might go, how much time we had left.

My opportunities to see Alan rolled around every other week but lasted for only half an hour. It was a system of rationing necessary so that all the families with relatives at the facility would have their fair turn, in keeping with Covid open-air and social distance compliance. The size of the patio, never intended for a pandemic, limited the number of visits. Even if a wrought-iron fence stood between us, though, I treasured any time I was able to spend with my husband.

In mid-October of 2020, Cathy arranged for a long weekend away from work so she could fly out and see her dad. As a teacher, it was especially difficult for her to make such a trip because flying with exposure to other passengers was risky, and she would need to be quarantined for two weeks upon her return. But we knew this visit might be her last chance to see her father.

I was also somewhat concerned for her sake, because too often Alan had been barely responsive, so I asked the facility whether, coming from so far and for such a short time, Cathy might be granted two visits. At best, I said, only one might be successful. They agreed to bend the rules.

By this time, I had worked out a few things: I knew morning appointments worked best. I thought the half-clear mask helped, and I also had the arias on my iPhone if Cathy wanted to use music as a way to get his attention. So we were all set.

After her flight, Cathy checked into a nearby hotel to minimize my exposure, and the next day, with both of us wearing masks, I drove her to the facility. I didn't want to infringe on her time with her dad, so after we reached the patio, I stood a few feet away and out of sight.

During her first morning visit, he was distracted and stared toward the side, then closed his eyes. A two-thousand-mile disappointment. But at least she saw him in person. The second visit was better. He became alert and listened while she again carried on a one-sided conversation about her life and home and the grandchildren. This time he even made eye contact with her.

Now it occurred to me that the key to awakening his attention might be sound, and one of his daughter's distinctive qualities was her cheerful voice. Perhaps hearing it helped him press through the fog of dementia and reach into the depths of memory. Maybe he recalled the sound imprint, if not the face, of the girl, the woman, he had raised and loved unconditionally for all of her fifty-six years. Maybe that was why he made eye contact.

Though I only had a quarter century, not a half century, of love between us, I had the arias. Cathy had her voice. Voices would soon become more important than I could ever imagine.

By November, the local monarch season was over, and the butterflies had completed their migration to over-wintering sites.

I was scheduled to see Alan twice that November. I came prepared by adding two new arias to a playlist that already included Pavarotti, Andrea Bocelli, and Maria Callas. During our half hour visit, Alan didn't act distracted. He didn't close his eyes. He maintained eye contact, and because I assumed he was enjoying the concerts, I was relaxed and less anxious about his antics, unlike the first visit when the water had been sprayed in my direction. I was glad for what seemed the return of a friendly routine.

Then, three days before Thanksgiving, I was allowed an extra visit. I decided to bring Pavarotti and friends along. I'd conjure other place names from our travels. It would be in the morning, his best time, and it would be with Katie as his caregiver escort, the one I called my Alan whisperer. Yet despite these ideal conditions, when that day came I could not make a connection with him. He looked to the side, closed his eyes, and seemed withdrawn. I drove home, dejected.

Two days later, on Thanksgiving, my spirits lifted when I was included in a long and cheerful Zoom call with Cathy, her husband, and the two grandkids who were home from college. Our granddaughter Sarah told me she wanted to try a Face Time call with her grandpa, even though she understood that he probably wouldn't know her. I said the best way would be if I made the video call to her during one of my scheduled patio visits.

Sarah was twenty-two now, and Alan's memory, at best, was trapped in snapshots of the distant past. To offset this, I planned to load my iPhone with photos of her at different ages, then hand the phone through the fence to his caregiver so she could show him those images before I placed the call.

After a bit of juggling to work around Sarah's online class schedule and the two-hour difference with the Midwest, we set a day and a time. It occurred to me that our granddaughter also has a distinctive voice, so I thought perhaps a fleeting recognition of her might occur, after all. I hoped it would for her sake; hoped that he might respond with his old familiar greeting to the women he loved in his family. We hoped he would say what we hadn't heard in a long time: "Hello, sweets."

I booked the patio visit for the morning of December 15.

The memory care facility was justly proud of its health record in the pandemic. Whereas many long-term care and memory care facilities had Covid cases and deaths among residents or staff, for the first ten months of 2020, this location of Westwinds had experienced none, a perfect but fragile record. Then, in late fall, one staff member tested positive.

And though until this point regulations had barred any family member from going inside a nursing or memory care facility, the health department had recently modified its rules. It now made an exception under one special circumstance. That exception was offered to me on December 7, when I received a call from a senior administrator at the facility. I was told that my husband was experiencing a rapid decline. How much time did he have left? Maybe a day, maybe a few. With his passing immanent, I would be permitted to enter the facility and go to his room, though I would have to wear full Personal Protective Equipment and sign a disclaimer. I immediately agreed.

This personal visit would be my first chance in eight months to touch my husband, and because he had only days or maybe only hours left, at last there would be no wrought-iron fence between us. I thought that once I was inside his room, then to hell with gloves at this point. For a moment I would hold his hand. I would lift my mask to kiss his cheek.

I was told I could receive a call at any time, that I would need to be ready to drive to the facility, twenty minutes away, as soon as the call came in.

It is difficult to describe how bittersweet it felt to hear this, such good news hinging on such terrible news. I wanted to be admitted to his room, to be near him, I could hardly wait, even though my impatience for this opportunity was linked to the fact that he was near death.

I cleared the calendar of my few commitments. I hung a few clothes easy to grab with hangars hooked on the front of the closet door in case a call should come in the middle of the night. I began my vigil.

About two days later, or maybe three because time starts to blur and I had stopped keeping track, the phone rang. I saw the phone identification for the facility and thought, *this is it, grab your car keys and go now.* But it wasn't.

I heard that my husband had tested positive for Covid. He would have to be isolated from the other patients. I would no longer be able to see him as agreed.

And I knew *this meant never.*

When I heard this, I became so distraught, so crazy over the conflict, the whiplash, because here I was, poised like a coiled spring ready to fly out the door and be with him and hold him and tell him I love him, and say goodbye ... and I had already told

Cathy I would have a chance to do this, and that I would do this for both of us, be her surrogate ... but now this was dashed, crashed, and I couldn't even bring myself to tell her.

Hysterical. There's no other word for it. But at least I had the presence of mind to call my best friend Pam, and she talked me through it, told me *You must tell Cathy*, and so I did, and Cathy and I cried together on the phone, and it seemed there was nothing more we could do.

Alan was in isolation for the next three or four days, and I received frequent updates from the hospice staff. He was not on a respirator but was on oxygen to aid his breathing, on antibiotics to fight back the infection and avoid further complications. He was on morphine. Keeping him comfortable was the goal of care.

We knew the end was near. Cathy asked me if a nurse would be willing to hold a phone to her father's ear so she could say goodbye, and I wanted to do this, too. We were told yes. But we didn't have much time left to make it work, not enough time for me to coordinate with a hospice nurse to make it happen. Cathy was two time zones away, and my phone number, but not hers, was linked to the nursing staff.

We turned to an intermediate step: an audio recording. Cathy recorded her message on her dad's iPhone, which I still had, and I made the arrangements with the nursing staff. My call would be live, and I would play her message into my phone.

The phone call is live now, the nurse holding a phone to his ear. I speak directly to him ... tell him I love him ... how he has been a *wonderful husband and lover and friend, then I play Cathy's message into my phone, I hear her musical voice, as if she is standing beside him, too, and this is what we do on December 14.*

The next day, the original date when we had planned for Alan's granddaughter to see him on FaceTime, though that won't happen now, Sarah also wants to give him her parting message. She records her message on Alan's phone, and with the help of the hospice nurse on the other end, I also play her message through my phone. It is one in the afternoon.

I'm told that hearing is one of the last remaining senses in a person who is dying, a last source for human contact. Alan's final sounds would be his granddaughter. An hour later, I receive another call. My husband has passed away.

Chapter 11
AFTER ALAN

An Alumna in the Alzheimer's Suport Group

THEY CALL DEMENTIA the long goodbye. They say we experience anticipatory grief. Both are true, but they don't relieve us of the pain and despair that descend like a downpour at the end. Mourning gives rise to a muddled time out of time. Bereavement induces a kind of insanity. Living alone, I sometimes heard my own voice cry out in primal keening sounds, as if human evolution reverses when facing the mystery of death.

I've been grateful for the kindness and support and the long telephone calls with family and old friends, and especially Cathy, for we share the loss of her father, and we are in constant touch in our sorrow. Though working two thousand miles apart, together we created a photographic memorial website celebrating Alan's life. In a pandemic era when so many miles separate us, I think the memorial website helps give the family comfort and closure.

After December 15, I became one of the alumni members of the Alzheimer's group. I turned to my group for grief support. A different kind of closure came from knowing that every week I would find solace in those two hours I could spend with my group, which by now had been meeting remotely for nine months. And maybe it's better that it took place on Zoom, because I only had to pull myself together, turn on the computer, and click an internet link, and there were the faces of friends who knew the pain of the long goodbye.

Some of them had gone from caregivers to alumni by now, too, and many had been with me almost from the beginning of my dementia journey.

During those mid-December meetings on the screen of my laptop, I had little to say at first. I felt raw, didn't trust my voice not to break up, and when it did, they soothed me. Eventually I would pull out of the fog of ambush sobbing and become a rational being and contribute again by sharing my own lessons learned. But not for a while. Then, because it was the holiday season, the group decided to have its first brief, masked, in-person and socially distanced gathering.

The occasion was a holiday cookie exchange at a large but shuttered art gallery belonging to the daughter of one of our members. Perhaps calling it a cookie exchange is a misnomer, though, because two of the members were experienced bakers and they provided us with all the goodies—decorated cookies, muffins, brownies, home-canned jam. A bounty assembled in festive carry-away bags with handles.

I arrived and accepted my bag and expressed my gratitude, but I didn't stay very long. Being newly a widow, I didn't want to be a downer. I had been in a daze that sunny, crisp winter day, and it was so soon, only a few days since Alan's passing. In fact, that same day I was driving to Westwinds to retrieve his wedding ring, which the facility director had in a drawer in her office for safekeeping.

I would rediscover when I got home with the bag—much as I had found that first time I visited Alan at Westwinds, when I'd been handed a box with a whole apple pie—how much that part of us we call the soul is calmed and consoled by receiving a gift of food. Today it was holiday cookies.

Now it is two months later, and the generous bakers in the Alzheimer's support group have spearheaded a second socially distant, face-to-face holiday gathering. This will be in celebration of Valentine's Day, but it will take place the day after, on the fifteenth, which happens to be our wedding anniversary.

The senior center where we formerly met in pre-pandemic times is still closed, but its director has given our organizers permission to set up a table and chairs in the parking area to accommodate a dozen or so people. Even though we will be wearing masks and sitting six feet apart, I look forward to this outing with folks who have become my friends through shared adversity. In case of inclement weather, we will meet under the senior center's overhanging porch roof.

For the bereaved, holidays and anniversaries loom like incoming dark clouds, especially if they, if we, live alone. The coincidence of this meeting taking place on my anniversary seems like a joyous distraction. It occurs to me that the caregiver's advice I'd tried to follow while caring for Alan—*Something to do, something to look forward to*—applies to me in this new chapter of my life.

I arrive and see the folding chairs arranged in a cautious semicircle. The table covered with a line-up of festive paper bags. These are for toting home a cornucopia of Valentine's delights from our bakers and canners: I see jars of jewel-toned, home-canned jams. I see decorated heart-shaped cookies peeking out of ribbon-tied, cellophane bags. Other cello bags printed with hearts hold brownies and miniature lemon muffins.

The star of the display, one for each of us, is a heart-shaped sugar cookie almost two inches tall and nearly as wide as the palm of my hand. It is decorated with white frosting and pink hearts and piped-on curlicues, and when you take off its top, you see that it is really four cookies. One forms the lid, and the other three are hollowed out to form a perfect center filled with the old-fashioned candy hearts, the kind kids give to little friends. Later, I would take them out and read them like runes: *Be Mine, Kiss me, Rock Star, Cute, Laugh, Let's Hug,* and one that said it all, *Miss you.*

But reading the candies came later, and in that moment at the senior center I stood in appreciative awe. This outpouring had taken so much time and thought and creativity on their part, and befriending these two giving people and the others, getting to know them, much less receiving these perks, had been (and would continue to be) a gift to me from this dementia journey.

Seeing everyone not on Zoom but in person felt fresh, and the novelty infused energy into conversations. Sometimes they were going on between two different clusters of people at once, impossible without tech gyrations on Zoom, and this was far from the only unexpected bit of interaction on this day.

At one point, we began showing pictures of grandkids and pets we had on our phones. One of our members showed us her adult daughter's pooch, her "grand-dog," and I remembered that I had images of monarchs on my phone. I scrolled through and found several, then chose one with a story behind it.

"Here is a newly emerged monarch," I told the group, "but it came out of its chrysalis the wrong way." I told them how a monarch usually emerges slowly, then clings to the chrysalis in a vertical position while setting its wings. "This one landed on the driveway, flat on her side, helpless. We wanted to do an intervention."

I told them how I had picked her up while Alan ran inside and grabbed a special item we always kept by the back door. Before dementia took over, he had designed this butterfly rescue tool: a temporary perch made of tissue, cardboard, and wire. The photograph showed a monarch, her claspers gripping the perch, her wings spread so they could dry in the perfect form.

"She sat there for an hour or so," I said, "then she flew away to find a mate."

"That's a clever invention on his part," someone said, and it gripped my heart to think of Alan, but not with the raw pain of our cookie event two months ago. This was a gentler feeling now, remembering the fallen butterflies this perch had saved. I felt a sense of pride for all he was, and for how we had worked together to help the monarchs survive. And I was grateful for everything we had shared, especially on this day of our anniversary.

A Souvenir of Sunset Views

OH, ALAN, you must have imagined that our tree house would stay forever young.

When you were growing up in a small Chicago apartment, you had no branches to scramble up and down. You had no notion of the joys—and the unexpected woes—such a whimsical structure might bestow should you someday become a homeowner.

Then, lo and behold, in 1990 and shortly before we met, you bought a home that came with that huge ash tree in the front yard, one so towering that in 1994 when O.J. Simpson went on his infamous Ford Bronco chase on the freeway near your new house, this tree was visible in the background of TV footage. You would dine out on that story for years to come.

When our grandkids were born—first a girl, then eighteen months later a boy, and never mind that they lived in Illinois—you decided the stout branches begged for a tree house, a hideaway for a latter-day Peter Pan. Now you had an excuse.

I knew your heart was set on this project, so I pushed back gently. "Of course ... the kids will outgrow it."

"Not until they go to college," you replied.

I negotiated. "Then why don't you build it without a roof? That way it can be used by adults, maybe for sunset cocktails."

That's how building that tree house became a multipurpose plan. After finding a carpenter willing to take on the job, you worked up the design and cleared hurdles about height and privacy and liability.

Our tree house turned out like a beautiful piece of furniture. It seemed to hover, almost floating in the air. From spring through fall, the slim wooden columns of its graceful railing sat nestled among a green bower of boughs. When the tree shed its leaves around the winter solstice, and the solitary structure stood out in bold relief, it provided an excellent display platform for lighted holiday decorations. And after the holidays, the annual cycle would begin again.

For a decade, when our grandkids visited, even if they didn't spend lot of time being arboreal during summer vacations, they sometimes read and snoozed in a hammock we kept up there. We adults had wine-and-sunset viewing parties in the tree house for six people, max. Usually the guests were close neighbors, including members of our co-ed book club.

And sometimes on a beautiful day, especially in those early years, you and I would scramble up the ladder and hoist up a picnic, then sit back in a pair of folding chairs we also stored up there and enjoy the sight from above. On those occasions, we'd see firsthand how it lured other Peter Pans, when a car pulled over to the curb and its driver looked up. If he didn't see us I'd call down, "Hello, we're up here" and I'd hear a response such as, "Great tree house!" I figured he'd always wanted one of his own.

Or sometimes the curious driver took it further. The doorbell rang and there stood a dad seeking the inside scoop on how to build a tree house like ours. On a rare occasion, if a kid begged his parents and the dad rang our bell, you would agree and take a child up the ladder and through the hatch. You two would climb up and look down, a guarantee of grins, waves, and laughter as if you were boys who happened to come in two different sizes.

By now, the tree house has presided over our front lawn for more than two decades. You might say it has seen better days. The wooden railing has termites, poor thing, and creaking joints, too, as I noticed when I was up there recently. Unlike the tree, or us for that matter, the structure does not grow new surface layers. Fresh concentric rings are not added to its lifespan.

The grandkids are now in college in the Midwest, their childhood summers behind us. And you are gone.

Somehow I'll need to take action this year, either replacing a large part of the timbers or simply tearing the whole thing down.

Neither of us anticipated facing this decision when we built our tree house, but I think that is largely true of how we all plan our lives. We don't want to live in a constant end-game state of mind. We go forth, try something, take a chance, and hope for the best. We intend to fare well and prosper.

After all considerations, it looks now like the tree house will be demolished, and that makes me sad. It's like an unfair payment on optimism has come due. A kind of pre-nostalgia sets in, though it is still there commanding its airy space. Or is this guilt I feel? If the tree house could talk it might say, *Hey, I gave my all for your family's best years.* I suppose I would reply that in exchange it has enjoyed—as you and I have enjoyed—a good, long run.

"Take plenty of pictures before you tear it down," your daughter says.

"Take several photographs," says a real estate broker. "Someone might want to build another one for their child. This way they can see what it looked like."

This prospect is not hard to imagine, even if the structure is absent. One of the thick center branches of the trunk was sliced off to create a stable foundation for construction. Removal will leave a gap tooth for a few months, but the tree is an expert at sprouting and colonizing its greenery. Soon it will inhabit the sunny space near its center and extend its far perimeter, including the top branches once famously visible from the freeway.

While the ash tree is reaching inward and skyward at the same time, down here on the ground we humans will adapt to change and loss, even as, like the tree limbs, we seek future growth and a clear path forward.

Chapter 12
A MONARCH EPILOGUE

I'D LIKE TO RETURN to the incident when I rescued the newbie butterfly trying to emerge, the one with an antenna stuck inside its chrysalis.

Alan and I had taken similar steps many times since 2013 when we saw a monarch in some kind of trouble. But as of a few months earlier, and unknown to me, it meant that on that spring day in 2021 I had broken a new law intended to protect monarchs: California Fish and Wildlife Service, Section 1002. It had gone into effect in my state, and was first posted online, on December 15, 2020. That coincided with the day I lost Alan.

Soon I learned more about this new regulation for protecting monarchs. Among its many provisions, it prohibited handling or touching them. That applied broadly to home gardeners, meaning any of us who are not employed by an accredited scientific institution. Nor is it sufficient to register a home garden with one of the monarch-supporting nonprofit organizations, although I hope someday a citizen certification will be possible.

I knew that I would have trouble complying with the no-handling rule. I also knew that I am not alone in wanting to push back. Tens of thousands of us from coast to coast and throughout the Midwest have spent years involved in providing milkweed, nectar plants, shelter and sometimes crisis care for the monarchs that we welcome to our front, back, and side yards. The largest monarch Facebook group, Beautiful Monarch, had around seventy-thousand members from around the nation who posted photographs, asked questions, and shared information. The California no-touch regulation—and the law is on track for federal enactment—caused such a reaction in this group that the moderator of this vast FB group halted discussion because of the heated nature of this topic.

Naturally we all are concerned about the monarch as an endangered species, and it deserves to be listed. The migration numbers of Eastern Monarchs, which start their journey in Canada and overwinter (during the season of suspended growth) in Mexico, have plummeted in recent years. The Western Monarchs that overwinter in California's Central Coast, like those Alan and I cared for, are in steep decline. And yes, listing monarchs will be beneficial in many ways, such as moderating expansion of agriculture and commercial development that would otherwise eradicate wide swaths of milkweed and nectar plants.

Meanwhile in our back yards, what should we do in the face of this well-intentioned and necessary regulation that comes with it a troublesome sub-rule about no touching?

I had a conversation recently at one of the outdoor events that promote native plant education and better stewardship of the planet. The individual happened to work in an outreach capacity for a highly respected wildlife nonprofit. I brought up what I believe is the need for nuance in this particular monarch protection rule. Organizations like his encourage citizens to plant milkweed and nectar plants at home. "But how," I asked, "can we sit back when we see a caterpillar, butterfly or chrysalis in trouble?"

I pointed out that there are many scenarios of how this might occur: What if a caterpillar wanders onto the driveway and is at risk of being smashed by a tire? I say move it. Okay, maybe I can use a stick or a leaf to, technically, not touch it. Or what if one forms its chrysalis where it will be slammed in a garage door? When this happened twice at our home I carefully detached it and with needle and thread, or using a tiny alligator clip, reattached it in a safe spot.

We were alone at the exhibit booth, and he seemed to listen closely as I made my case. "Well, California Poppies are protected," the outreach rep said. "You can't pick them in nature or public areas or even touch them. But what if some poppies happen to grow in your own back yard?"

I left feeling somewhat reassured by this comparison. I think I can comply with the law, for the most part. Shifting to more container gardening is one way, so I can move a potted milkweed near a caterpillar when it strips another plant bare and runs out of food. I can semi-comply by using the stick- or leaf-carry if I need to relocate one from harm's way.

And yet ... after participating in hours of online discussions about monarchs since 2022, I have learned there are reasons not to always help them survive, times when it is best to let nature take its course, though it may seem counterintuitive not to help them. For example, after emerging from its chrysalis, and after a reasonable length of time for the wings to expand and dry, if a butterfly is still twisted … then it cannot be coaxed to fly. Nor should it reproduce and carry forth damaged genes. Or if a plump caterpillar in a hanging J (the position it takes just before forming its chrysalis) goes skinny and slack, it is doomed by parasites you cannot see. The best thing one can do in either of these cases is ignore them or deliver the coup de gras, as I have learned to do. A hard lesson, but it is part of the love I give them.

I wish I could tell Alan about the fascinating information I am learning. I'd want him to know how his suggestion from years ago to diversify our milkweed has become central to my monarch gardening. How I am more deeply involved with monarch education, including participating in Citizen Science. So far, in one year, our Monarch Monitoring group, under the aegis of the Aquarium of the Pacific, has sponsored or contributed to the planting of milkweed and nectar plants in two public parks in Long Beach.

But mainly I am a backyard butterfly gardener.

If you'd asked us back in 2013 when we began our monarch adventure: Should monarch butterflies be protected by the Endangered Species Act (under Fish and Wildlife Services) Alan and I wouldn't have paused before saying *Yes, of course.*

Now I will follow the law, maybe with a little twist.

I've replaced the tropical milkweed in my garden, and I'm learning the tricky technique of raising native narrow leaf from seed, which Alan and I could not figure out how to do. I'm experimenting with Showy milkweed, which has wide leaves, roomy enough for chubby fourth-instar caterpillars. And narrow leaf, which starts out skimpy as a seedling but becomes more robust after making its spring rebound in succeeding years.

For seven years, monarch butterflies and their caterpillars were entwined in our marriage, in our lives, the last four as therapy and distraction while I cared for my husband.

I intend to carry on our tradition, coming up with practical workarounds and, yes, the occasional intervention, so the monarch butterflies and their caterpillars will continue to play a vital and healing role in my life, and I will in theirs.

Acknowledgments

I AM DEEPLY GRATEFUL to the leaders and members of my Alzheimer's Association support group. I hope I have conveyed the coping and healing power of our shared experiences.

Similarly, I am indebted to the kind and professional caregivers noted in this memoir, whose names were changed to respect their privacy. The word *heroes* aptly describes them, especially during the long months of Covid crisis for us all.

The Floral Park neighborhood association in Santa Ana provided a much-needed distraction and a purposeful project soon after I lost Alan, when I participated in establishing a butterfly garden in a public park one block from our home. In June of 2021 I assisted Chris Switzer with the celebratory opening of the butterfly garden in Sarah May Downie Herb Garden.

I want to thank my writers' critique group, Pam Tallman, PJ Penman and Terry Black. They helped me sharpen this memoir, often on Zoom, as I tried to capture moments of life in real time. Thanks, too, to book industry veteran Pam Sheppard and editor Barbara Ardinger, who helped move this project forward, as well as to Dr. Ed Kaufman for early-draft manuscript insights, and Todd Crashaw, for his beautiful cover design.

Finally, and most essentially, I want to express my gratitude to Cathy. I do not know how I would have survived this journey without your caring support.

Monarchs 101

antennae—'feelers' or long appendages on the head of an adult butterfly for balance and sensing smells

button—knob of silk the pre pupa attaches to

chrysalis—hard case where caterpillar changes to a butterfly

cremaster—a stem by which a pupa or chrysalis hangs

diapause—period of seasonally suspended growth

eclose—emerge or come out of chrysalis

frass—caterpillar excrement

hatch—from egg

instar—growth stages of a caterpillar

larva—caterpillar stage

milkweed—a family of perennial herbs

molt—shedding of skin between stages or instars

OE—*ophryocystis elektroscirrha,* a protozoan parasite

overwintering—when monarchs remain inactive

oviposit—to lay an egg

pre-pupa—hanging in J shape

proboscis—flexible tube on butterfly for sipping nectar

pupa—chrysalis stage

pupate—go from caterpillar to chrysalis

swarm—a group of butterflies

Tachinid fly —a predator that lays eggs in a caterpillar

Tarsal claw—main claw of the butterfly at the end of its leg

tentacles—appendages supplying sensory information for caterpillar, often mistaken for antennae

About the Author

Allene Symons is a former senior editor for *Publishers Weekly* magazine in New York. She has written articles, essays, reviews, and columns for business and consumer magazines and newspapers, including the *Los Angeles Times*. She earned a bachelor's in philosophy from San Francisco State University and master's degrees in the fields of Communications (Journalism) from CSU Fullerton and in History of Religions (Buddhism) from Claremont Graduate University. She currently lives in Long Beach, California.

Other books by Allene Symons

Aldous Huxley's Hands: His Quest for Perception and the Origin and Return of Psychedelic Science (Prometheus Books, 2015).

Adventures Abroad: Exploring the Travel Retirement Option, co-author with Jane Parker (Gateway Books/ Globe Pequot 1991).

Nostradamus, Vagabond Prophet: A Novel of His Life and Times (Avon Books 1983; reissued by Forked Road Press 2011).

9 780980 116588